Off the Wall

Photographs by Phil Bath
Drawings by Dick Kohfield

Off the Wall
Championship Racquetball
for the Ardent Amateur

Charles Brumfield
Five Times National Champion

Jeffrey Bairstow

The Dial Press
New York

Published by
The Dial Press
1 Dag Hammarskjold Plaza
New York, New York 10017

Manufactured in the United States of America

Third Printing—1981

Library of Congress Cataloging in Publication Data

Brumfield, Charles.
  Off the wall.

  Includes index.
  1. Racquetball. I. Bairstow, Jeffrey, 1939–
joint author. II. Title.
GV1017.R3B78   796.34   78-8031
ISBN 0-8037-7272-6
ISBN 0-8037-7274-2 pbk.

In Memoriam PHILIP BATH

This book would not have been possible without the zeal and creative enthusiasm of Phil Bath. Phil, who photographed the high-speed action sequences used in this book, died before he could see the printed results of his work.

We wish to dedicate this book to his memory.

Charles Brumfield and Jeffrey Bairstow

Contents

Off the Wall

1

The Game of Racquetball

It's almost surrealistic, in a way. Imagine being locked in a brightly lit, white wooden room about forty feet long, twenty feet high and twenty feet wide. You and your opponent are dressed for tennis but are wielding stubby racquets that look like oversized table-tennis bats with strings and the ball is a hairless black instead of a fuzzy yellow. You bounce the ball and prod it toward the front wall. It bounces obligingly back. Your opponent takes a healthy swipe and the ball caroms off three walls, forcing you to run around like a captured chicken. You whale at the ball and it zaps the front wall with a resounding *splat* and then screams past your opponent's outstretched racquet for a winner.

That's racquetball. And, what's more, the player who won that last point could be you within a few minutes of stepping inside the racquetball court.

Racquetball is a fast-moving sport that's entirely in tune with contemporary life. It's easily learned by young and old, women and men. It's fast, exciting and competitive and has an element of risk. It provides a great deal of healthy exercise in a relatively small physical space and in a short period of time. As your skills improve, so does the game, which remains constantly challenging no matter what the level of your play. Both equipment and court-time are relatively cheap, and the game is exciting

Why Racquetball?

to watch. In short, I can't think of a better sport.

Racquetball resembles squash, and already has even more participants. In fact, Vic Niederhoffer, a former national squash champion, claims that, "In ten years, racquetball will be bigger than tennis." I'll drink to that. When I started to play serious racquetball in the late 1960's there were fewer than a hundred thousand players, mostly in Southern California. Now there are more than five million players scattered over the entire United States. There are also national championships for all age groups and professional tours for both men and women.

If you have never played racquetball before, I hope this book will serve as an introduction to the sport and get you out on a court fast. If you are already a player, the advice and instruction I'm offering here will help you refine your strokes and develop your court tactics and strategy. I hope this book will help you get as much pleasure and satisfaction from the sport as I have had as a racquetballer.

What Is Racquetball? Racquetball is a court sport played with a short-handled racquet that has a smaller head than a tennis racquet, a soft rubber ball and rules somewhat similar to those of squash or handball. Although there are three-wall and one-wall versions of racquetball, the most popular game is played on a four-wall court (see diagram) with a wooden floor and hard walls and ceiling.

The court is divided into two halves (the front court and back court) by the short line—a line drawn across the court midway between the front and back walls. A second line, called the service line, is drawn across the court five feet in front of the short line. To begin play, the server stands in the service zone formed by the short and service lines, bounces the ball and hits it so that the ball strikes the front wall and bounces back to land behind the short line—any serve not doing so is said to be "short." The server is allowed two attempts at service. If the server double faults, the opponent then serves.

If the serve is good, the receiver then returns the ball by hitting it before the second bounce. The return must hit the front wall before touching the floor for the ball to stay in play. The players then hit the ball alternately until a fault occurs. If a player's shot fails to hit the front wall, or the player fails to hit the ball before it bounces twice on the floor, that player loses the point. Points are awarded only to the server. If the server loses the point, then he loses the right to continue serving and the receiver then serves.

Game in racquetball is twenty-one points. The first player to reach twenty-one wins the game—there is no deuce point as in tennis. The first player to win two games wins the match, but if the score is one game all, a third eleven-point "tiebreaker" game is played.

Another important rule requires you to allow your opponent a clear view of the ball. After the ball is hit, you must move to permit the other player a clear shot at the ball. If you deliberately do not do so, then your opponent can claim an "avoidable hinder" and you lose the point. If one player unavoidably gets in the way of another, an "unavoidable or dead ball hinder" can be claimed and the point replayed. In ordinary play, the players will have to decide hinders for themselves. In tournament play, the referee will call and make all such decisions.

A full set of racquetball rules (see Appendix) is available for fifty cents from the United States Racquetball Association, 4101 Dempster Street, Skokie, Illinois 60076. Membership in the U.S.R.A. costs only five dollars per year and includes a free rule book, tournament eligibility and a subscription to *National Racquetball Magazine.* The magazine, which is published twelve times a year, contains much useful instructional material and news of developments in professional and amateur racquetball. It's well worth the money.

Most racquetball play is singles with only two players on the court. Doubles is a spectacularly fast and furious game that I would not recommend for the beginning player. However, once you have good court skills and ball awareness, doubles can be a lot of fun. I'll be talking about doubles in detail in Chapter 7.

How Did Racquetball Begin? The "invention" of racquetball is generally credited to Joe Sobek, a professional tennis and squash teacher from Greenwich, Connecticut. Back in 1950, Sobek decided that the game of paddleball, played in an enclosed handball court with a soft rubber ball and a wooden paddle, might be easier if a strung racquet were used instead. Sobek's new sport caught on in Greenwich but spread rather slowly, mostly by word of mouth, to a few other parts of the country.

The sport had established a number of strongholds in the Middle and Far West by 1969, when a San Diego dentist, Dr. Bud Muehlheisen, and a few other racquetball fanatics staged the first national racquetball tournament at the Jewish Community Center in St. Louis—then, as now, a hotbed of racquetball activity. From that tournament there arose the International Racquetball Association under the guiding hand of Chicago real-estate millionaire Bob Kendler, at the time the president of the United States Handball Association. He is now the driving force behind the United States Racquetball Association and its pro offshoot, the National Racquetball Club.

Despite its origins in the East, the sport first really caught on in Southern California, San Diego in particular. That was partly because San Diego has always had a concentration of fanatics like Bud Muehlheisen and partly because the major racquet manufacturer, Leach Industries, is based there. From California, the sport has gradually spread back eastward to the point that some estimates now suggest that there are about a hundred thousand courts and five million players across the nation. There are courts in almost every major city and racquetballs' invasion of the suburbs is rivalling the spread of indoor tennis clubs.

Strangely enough, the spread of the sport has been slowest in the Northeast, where it was invented. This is probably due to the innate conservatism of Easterners, the relative strength of squash in that part of the country and the lack of courts. However, courts are now being opened in both New York City and in Boston and it can only be a short time before the sport becomes as popular in the East as it is in the rest of the country.

Equipment has much improved over the past few years (see Chapter 8) and racquets and balls are now available everywhere. In the early 1970's Leach Industries was turning out ten thousand racquets a year; now the company makes over five hundred thousand. The leading maker of balls, Seamco, sold over six million in 1977 and can hardly keep up with the demand. I think it's safe to say that racquetball is fast becoming a very popular sport.

2

The Forehand and Backhand Drives

The racquetballer's forehand drive is both the workhorse stroke on which his game is based and the flashy killing stroke that satisfies his ego and elicits murmurs of approval from the spectators' gallery. Unlike most other racquet sports, the backhand drive in racquetball is generally less useful than the forehand. For most players, power comes more naturally on the forehand side, and therefore a racquetballer should concentrate on developing the forehand drive.

This is not to say that the backhand can be neglected. There will be many occasions when you will have to use a backhand drive and more than a few when you will win the points with it. When you are playing in the back court, the area where most drives are hit, I recommend the "sword and shield" approach. Use your backhand as a shield—the defensive shot that will keep the point going. Use your forehand as a sword—the shot that will win you the point immediately.

Work on your backhand until you have good ball control and can keep yourself out of trouble. Don't worry if you can't even approach the power of your forehand—neither can I. Just remember the sword and shield philosophy.

Before I show you how to hit both the forehand and backhand drives, I'd like to emphasize three fundamen-

The Fundamentals

tals which, if you're a beginner, you should force your-self to keep in mind every time you go out to play or practice. Of course by the time you become an intermediate player, they should already be instinctive.

First, and this applies to every single moment of racquetball play, watch the ball. This is not a matter of simply keeping a casual eye on the ball and hoping your concentration will increase when it's your turn to hit. Watch that ball as though you are expecting it to explode any second. Remember the ball will sometimes be moving very fast. The forehand kill shot of professional Steve Serot has been clocked at speeds well over a hundred miles per hour. Lose sight of the ball and most likely you've lost the point.

Second, always use the proper grip for each type of stroke. In the next few pages I'll be showing you those grips, but for now, I just want you to be aware of their importance. The wrong grip will not only limit your progress, it will take months to correct when you finally realize you are gripping the racquet badly. Start your racquetball play with the correct grips and they, too, will become so instinctive you'll be unaware of your grip changes as you switch from one shot to the next.

The third fundamental is to use your weight at all times—and I don't mean body blocking your opponent. Many racquetball situations call for the ball to be hit with all the power you can muster. If you rely on your arm and shoulder muscles to produce that power, not only will you be limiting yourself but you'll also be running the risk of early fatigue and serious injury. As in tennis or squash, you transfer your weight from your back foot to your front foot as you hit the ball. For many players, this will almost double the power of the shot. You do not have to be physically strong to be a good racquetball player, but you do have to know the proper mechanics of hitting the ball. Using your body is a vital part of every stroke.

If you find your game has suddenly gone sour, take a time-out and ask yourself if you are following the three fundamental principles I've just described. If not, make a special attempt to put the principles back into your game and, chances are, your losing streak will be stopped in its tracks.

 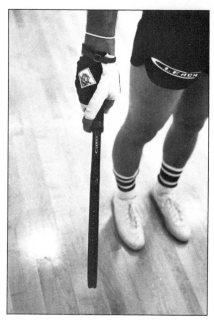

Forehand Grip

The Grips The objective of the two racquetball grips—the forehand and backhand—is to make the racquet an extension of your hand, so that the face of the racquet is always square to the ball's intended line of flight in the hitting zone. This may sound a little technical but it's really quite simple. If the racquet is facing in the direction you want the ball to go, then the ball will automatically go in that direction when you hit it. If your racquet face is not perpendicular to the direction in which you want the shot to go, that may be because your grip is incorrect.

The forehand racquetball grip is very similar to the tennis player's "shakehands" or "Eastern" forehand grip. Pick up the racquet with your other hand and hold it by the throat so that the face is perpendicular to the ground. Place the palm of your racquet hand on the strings and then slide it down until it is next to the handle. Now close your hand and "shake hands" with

Backhand Grip

the racquet. Spread your fingers so that the index finger is apart from the middle finger and bent to form a "trigger finger." Wrap your thumb around the grip until it touches your middle finger. The "V" formed by your thumb and index finger should be in the center of the top flat of the handle (see Photos).

The butt of the handle should stick out from your hand—in fact you should "choke up" slightly on the handle for the best wrist control. If you don't believe me, try the "waggle test." Hold the racquet with the butt inside your palm and try to waggle the racquet with your other hand. Now choke up on your grip and try again. If you are holding the racquet properly, you'll have more control with the choked grip.

Remember, too, that racquetball is a wristy game—a sharp wrist snap will add an extra edge of power to your shots, so you must grip the racquet with your fingers. (In fact, most of the gripping pressure will be in the last three fingers of your hand.) You can do this more easily than you would be able to do with a tennis racquet because racquetball grip sizes are smaller.

If you are a beginner, I suggest you check your grip after each practice shot and, if necessary, regrip the racquet each time. That way you'll be sure to forestall the potential bad habit of an incorrect grip. Of course, I wouldn't recommend that you regrip after every shot in a match—there just isn't time. Make your grip instinctive during your practice sessions and you won't go wrong when you play in a match.

Take the majority of your shots with the forehand grip. This grip is used for the serve, the forehand drive, the lob and volleys up against the front wall. However, you should change your grip for the backhand drive and the overhead (see Chapter 4). At first you'll need both hands to make the grip change but after a while you should be able to do it singlehandedly.

For a correct backhand grip, take up the usual forehand grip and, with your other hand, turn the racquet about one eighth of a turn away from your body. (This would be toward the right if you're right-handed, toward the left if you're left-handed.) This turn should put your hand on the top face of the handle with the first knuckle of your index finger in the center of that top face and the V of your thumb and index finger on the top left bevel of the grip (see Photo). Spread your fingers slightly, as with the forehand, and wrap your thumb around the grip.

Although it is rather tempting to do so, don't put your thumb up the back of the handle. This will only make you poke at your backhand and stop you from developing a good wrist snap. Keep that thumb wrapped around the handle.

This backhand grip may feel a little uncomfortable at first. However, as you begin to practice the stroke you'll realize that this grip position will keep the face of the racquet square to the intended line of flight of the ball as you make the hit, just as with the forehand. If you find your backhand shots are floating up in the air, check your grip. You'll probably find that you are not making the grip change from forehand to backhand.

Practice making the grip change as soon as you start your backswing for a backhand. Eventually the change should become automatic. Until that time, keep checking your grip.

1. Grip the racquet with your fingers, not the palm of your hand.

2. Choke up for better control.

3. Check the position of the V between your thumb and first finger.

4. Spread your fingers as though you were about to pull the trigger on a gun.

Grip Checklist

The Ready Position There are really two ready positions in racquetball. The first is the position you take when you are waiting for your opponent to hit the ball, the second when you are about to hit the ball yourself. For the sake of clarity, I'm going to call the first the ready position and the second the set-up position.

The ready position, which you adopt immediately after completing your own stroke and while waiting for your opponent to hit the ball, is essentially a crouch preparatory to moving into a hitting position. Hold the racquet level with your chest, ready to start your backswing. Your body should be flexed, with your knees bent, and most of your weight should be on your back foot, ready to push off in the direction in which you expect to hit the ball.

While waiting for your opponent to hit the ball you should be standing in a central court position about four feet behind the short line. As in squash, control of the center court position is one of the keys to winning. Stand with your body perpendicular to the front wall, facing the side on which you expect to hit the ball. Watch your opponent over your shoulder to minimize the risk of being hit in the face by the ball. As soon as your opponent hits the ball and you see what direction it's going in, get moving. If you wait until the ball bounces off the front wall, your stroke will be too late; you won't have enough time to make your decision. Move into position and hit the ball.

In some ways it's better to move, even in the wrong direction, than to postpone your decision. By breaking your inertia immediately after your opponent hits the ball, you are moving that fraction of a second earlier and changes of direction will be faster than if you started from a stationary position. Once in motion, you can change direction and flow quickly into the proper set-up position.

Estimating the best set-up position is one of the hardest things for a beginner. Ideally you should set up so that the ball will be about knee high when you make contact. Most often this means sidestepping backward and then moving forward into the shot. Practice and more practice will help you develop a feel for the ball's flight and your own position relative to that flight.

As you arrive in the set-up position you should be sideways to the line of flight of the ball, with your weight on your back foot and your racquet back at the top of the backswing. And, of course, your eyes should be glued to the approaching ball. Your body should be flexed, with the knees bent, but still maintaining good balance. If you are off balance as you set up, you will not be able to put your weight into the shot properly.

In the ready and set-up positions, the biggest mistakes made by beginners and intermediate players are (a) facing the front wall and (b) making decisions too late. A player who faces the front wall will simply take too long to get moving into position for the next shot. But it's no use being in a good ready position unless you decide quickly on your next move. In basketball the best player is the one who can play without the ball—the one who is making decisions all the time. In racquetball make your decisions before the ball reaches you.

Forehand Drive

1

2

3

The Forehand Drive Anyone who has played golf will soon recognize the principles of hitting a racquetball forehand drive. The racquet moves back and forward in a huge semi-circular arc, the hips and shoulders are rotated and the wrist is snapped at contact to put maximum power into the shot. The critical part of the forward drive, though, is the set-up—being in the right place, with the added complication of being there at exactly the right time.

The most effective point at which to make contact with the ball on a forehand drive is when the ball has dropped to approximately knee height. You must move behind the flight of the ball until you are in a position where a step to transfer your weight into the shot will bring your racquet and the ball together at knee height. It takes quite a lot of experience to judge the correct set-up position. If you already play another racquet sport you will probably have quite good judgment of the ball's flight path. If not, there's no substitute for lots of practice.

4   5   6

The moment you decide to take the next shot on your forehand side, start moving into the set-up position (Photo 1), taking your racquet back to the top of the backswing as you do so (Photo 2). When you get to your set-up position, your racquet should be all the way back, out of the line of flight of the ball. Your wrist should be cocked and your forearm should be at about a ninety degree angle to your upper arm (Photo 3). At this point your body should be flexed with most of your weight on your back foot so you can step into the ball. Naturally, your eyes should be watching the ball very closely.

As you start your forward swing, several things should happen simultaneously. Like a golfer, you should make a lateral movement of your hips and knees to initiate the weight transfer (Photo 4). Begin your shoulder rotation by bringing the shoulder of your racquet arm down so that as the racquet comes into the vertical plane, it will swing through to contact the ball. Step toward the ball to

7   8   9

widen your stance. At the same time use your other arm for balance, like a tightrope walker.

As your racquet swings forward, lead with your elbow, keeping your wrist laid back in a cocked position (Photo 5). The preparation for the forehand drive is rather like drawing back a rubberband—you are releasing the rubberband, but in stages, so as to build up to maximum racquethead speed as you make contact with the ball. Keep your forearm bent until the shoulder of your racquet arm is pointing toward the ground. Then, straighten out your arm so as to make contact with the ball at about knee height (Photo 6), somewhere between the center of your stance and the instep of your front foot.

As you make contact with the ball, almost all your weight should be on your front foot and your eyes should be watching the racquet face even though the ball may be moving too fast for you to see it actually hitting the racquet (Photo 7).

10

Start your wrist snap just before contact and allow the snap to continue until after the ball leaves the racquet. It is this snap that will put the extra edge of power into your shot. Again, the racquetball snap is very much like that of a golfer contacting the ball. As you hit the ball, your arm, wrist and racquet should be in a straight line to drive the ball on its way to the front wall (Photo 8).

After contact, don't deliberately slow your arm motion. Let the body continue to rotate and let your racquet follow through quite naturally (Photo 9). Your weight will now be mainly on your front foot but your body should still be bent low. Resist the temptation to come up as you complete the stroke. If you do straighten up, you'll most likely hit the ball up rather than low to the front wall. Your racquet should finish high on the other side of your body so that you are facing the front wall looking at the ball over your front shoulder.

However, don't just stand there and admire your flowing forehand. Move up to the commanding center court position while watching the ball, and get ready for your opponent's next move. Of course, if you've hit a successful forehand low to the front wall, you've probably hit a winner and the point will be over in your favor.

Forehand Drive Checklist

1. Get your racquet back early.
2. Move rapidly to your set-up position.
3. Watch the ball constantly.
4. Transfer your weight laterally as you hit.
5. Keep your body low throughout the stroke.
6. Carry through your wrist snap for maximum power.

Common Forehand Errors

1. No weight transfer. If you don't transfer your weight, you won't put enough power into the shot. Watch a baseball pitcher or a football player throw a ball and you'll see how important weight transfer is. Start with your weight on your back foot and begin the stroke with a hip and knee movement that will transfer the weight to your front foot.

2. Late preparation. If you don't get your racquet back as you set up for the ball, the backswing and the forward swing will become meshed together. The backswing will be too short and the forward swing will be a jerky motion instead of the long flowing arc that's really needed. The moment your timing seems to be off, ask yourself if you're getting your racquet back early enough. If not, start taking it back the moment your opponent hits the ball and you begin to move into position.

3. No chain reaction of body, arm and wrist. Too many beginning players swing almost exclusively with their arms, producing weak shots and, most likely, sore elbows. The forehand is like a chain reaction. The hips start the body moving, the shoulders rotate to continue the swing, the upper arm unwinds, the forearm straightens out and finally the wrist snaps to complete the reaction. Omit any part of that chain reaction and you are robbing your shot of vital power.

4. Failure to let the ball drop. Many players are so anxious just to hit the ball that they don't wait to let the ball drop to knee height or lower. If you hit the ball too high, it will strike the front wall too high and be an easier shot for your opponent to return. Hit the ball when it is six inches to a foot off the ground and you'll hit a winner. Patience is necessary, especially if you are nervous or anxious about hitting the ball.

Backhand Drive

1   2   3

The Backhand Drive Most players—myself included—have a harder time with the backhand drive than with the forehand. I know the physiology experts say a backhand should be a more powerful shot because the action extends your arm instead of crossing it in front of your body the way the forehand does. For all that, most of us have trouble in simply hitting a backhand, to say nothing of putting enough power into it. I think the problem is one of practice. We all begin by hitting forehands, so we tend to concentrate more practice time on them at the expense of the backhand. The answer to a weak backhand is to practice it more than the other strokes in your repertoire. Of course, if you are one of those lucky individuals who have better backhands than forehands, the reverse applies. Always practice your weakness.

The key to hitting any power shot is to get the face of the racquet square to the intended line of flight of the ball just before and during contact. You can do that only

4   5   6

if you have the proper backhand grip (see p. 12). Before you work on your backhand, practice changing your grip from the forehand to the backhand side. When you can make the change without using two hands and without looking at the racquet, then you're ready to work on your backhand. Remember that in a match your grip change and position must be instinctive. Get it right in your practice sessions and your grips will be automatic in match play.

When the ball comes to you on your backhand side, turn your body sideways to the line of flight of the ball (Photo 1) and get your weight back so that it is almost entirely on your back foot (Photo 2). Take the racquet back as rapidly as you can, cocking your wrist at the same time (Photo 3). As the ball approaches, flex your body, bend your knees and step toward the ball (Photo 4). As you swing your racquet forward and down, start moving your weight forward (Photo 5) to put some power

7   8   9

into the shot. Keep your wrist cocked for the essential wrist snap as you hit the ball but begin to straighten your forearm and elbow as you start the racquet's forward swing (Photo 6).

Make contact with the ball just ahead of your front knee, preferably when the ball is between one and two feet from the floor (Photo 7). At contact, your racquet face should be almost vertical, with the head at about wrist height. Don't let the racquet head droop or you'll scoop the ball upward, so that it will hit high on the front wall and provide an easy return for your opponent. Start your wrist snap just before you hit the ball and continue until after the ball has left your racquet (Photo 8). The action is rather like that of snapping a Frisbee. The more wrist you can put into the shot, the more power you'll develop.

Keep your follow-through low and in the direction you wish the ball to go (Photo 9) but allow your arm to swing

10

naturally across your body so that your finish is high in the air (Photo 10). Just as with the forehand drive, a full follow-through is essential for a powerful shot. Finishing high will ensure that you hit through rather than abruptly stopping the shot soon after the ball leaves your racquet. Too short a follow-through usually indicates that you are slowing down the racquet head through contact. In fact, the racquet head should be moving at its fastest during the contact and should not slow down until you are well into the follow-through.

Backhand Drive Checklist

1. Watch the ball.
2. Get your racquet back early.
3. Step into the shot to put your weight into it.
4. Bend your knees and upper body so that you make contact low.
5. Snap your wrist sharply through contact for extra power.
6. Finish your follow-through to make sure that you hit through the ball.

Common Backhand Errors

1. Not getting down to the ball. One of the keys to a good backhand drive is to hit the ball as low as possible. You can do that only if you get down to the ball by bending your knees and flexing your upper body. Don't drop the racquet head in order to reach the ball—bend your body.

2. Falling away from the ball. If you don't retreat early so that you can hit the ball low, you'll find that the ball may be waist high as you swing forward. This makes most players lean back as they hit the ball. The result is no forward weight shift, so very little power is put into the shot. In extreme cases, a player will lean back so far that he loses his balance. Get back behind the ball so that you can step into the shot.

3. Not hitting through the ball. If your backhand lacks any real power despite a step into the ball, the chances are that you are not hitting through the ball. The answer to this is usually a longer follow-through so that the racquet is moving at its fastest as you hit the ball. Check to make sure that you are finishing with your racquet high in the air. That way you'll increase the time that the racquet is in contact with the ball.

4. Little or no wrist snap. If you don't cock your wrist on the backswing, there's no way you'll be able to snap at the ball. Start cocking your wrist as you take the racquet back and hold that cocked position until just before you hit the ball. Then snap the wrist sharply through and after contact, just as though you were throwing a Frisbee.

3

The Serve

As in the other racquet sports, the serve in racquetball is perhaps the most important shot in a player's repertoire. Not only do you have complete control over placing the ball and timing your stroke, but you serve from the all-important and commanding center court position. By serving well, you will probably elicit a weak return and be in a great position to finish off the point with your next shot. Therefore, you should devote time to practicing and developing your serve and you should always think carefully about each serve you hit in a match.

To serve, a player must stand within the service zone (see diagram on page 30), bounce the ball within that zone and then hit the ball so that it rebounds from the front wall and lands in the court behind the short line. The receiver must stay at least five feet behind the short line and cannot return the ball until it crosses that line (although the receiver has the option of hitting the ball before it bounces).

A serve is a fault if: (a) it hits the floor before crossing the short line, (b) it hits the front wall and two side walls without bouncing on the floor, (c) it hits the ceiling, (d) it hits the back wall before bouncing on the floor, (e) it goes out of court (for example, through the spectators' gallery) or (f) the server commits a foot fault by stepping out of the service zone before the served ball crosses the

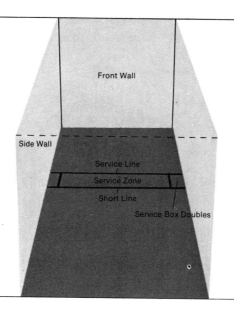

Front Wall

Side Wall

Service Line

Service Zone

Short Line

Service Box Doubles

short line. If the server double faults by hitting two faults in succession, then the server is said to be "hand-out" and the right to serve goes to the receiver.

A server can also be hand-out directly by hitting an out serve, such as a serve which fails to hit the front wall, a missed ball or a serve that touches the server on rebound. For precise details on fault and out serves, consult the rules (see Appendix).

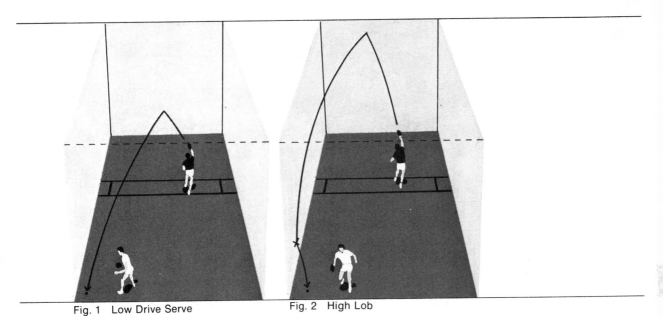

Fig. 1   Low Drive Serve   Fig. 2   High Lob

The key to effective serving, in my opinion, is not tremendous power or fantastically accurate placement (although both of these are very useful) but great variety. By varying the type, pace and placement of your serve you can always keep your opponent guessing. That way, the receiver can never get in a groove and the nervous tension that you create in your opponent will probably put him off his game enough to give you the upper hand when you are serving. That's the way it should be. You are in charge when you serve and you should expect to win the point.

I'm going to describe four basic serves in terms of the stroking you'll need and the strategies you should use with each one. The four serves are: the drive, which is hit low at the front wall, travels fast and bounces deep in the back court (see Fig. 1); the lob, which is hit high on the front wall, glances off the side wall, bounces and dies near the back wall (see Fig. 2); the "garbage," or half-lob, which carries just beyond the short line and

The
Four
Basic Serves

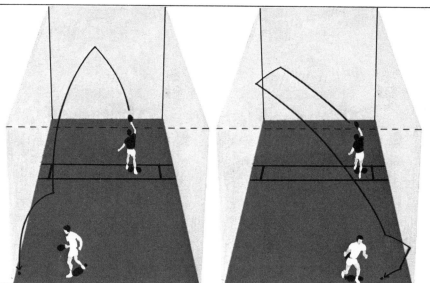

Fig. 3   Garbage Serve   Fig. 4   Z Serve

bounces in a relatively high arc to die at the back wall
(see Fig. 3); and the Z serve, which hits the front wall
near the corner, rebounds off the side wall and then
goes crosscourt to bounce on the floor just before hitting the opposite wall, thus describing a Z-shaped path
(see Fig. 4).

Each serve has its place in racquetball play and you
should try to become proficient in each type. Stroking a
served ball is easier than hitting a ball in play. In fact, the
strokes you'll need are very similar to the drives and lobs
that you use in play, so you should practice each type of
serve and, just as important, keep trying each one in
play. Too many players develop a favorite serve and stick
to it when the going gets rough. I'm always happy to face
an opponent like that because I can easily anticipate the
serve and hit a winning return.

Although I am going to concentrate on the four basic
serves, there's no reason why you shouldn't develop
some specialties of your own. It's worth experimenting

with the serve to see just what you can do with the ball. In fact, if you watch a pro racquetball tournament, you'll see many serves that are not in this or any other book. Those serves are the ones that give the receivers the most trouble, and that's what serving is all about—giving your opponent lots of trouble.

The Drive Serve The drive serve is the power weapon in your serve arsenal. Like the forehand drive, it should be hit low and hard at the front wall so that the ball stays low as it zooms into the back court. Ideally, the drive serve should be so low on the rebound that it will bounce twice before hitting the back wall. If you hit the drive serve too high, the ball will bounce and then fly off the back wall, where it will lose all its pace and hang there like a pumpkin to be blasted by your opponent.

There are two variations on the drive—the center court V drive and the wide V drive. For the center V drive, stand in the center of the service zone and aim the ball at a spot no more than three feet off the floor midway between the side wall and center of the front wall. If the ball is struck properly (see Fig. 1), it will rebound close to the side wall. This means your opponent, assuming that he has taken up a normal receiving position near the center of the court, must run the entire length of the rear side wall in an attempt to flag down your serve. In addition, the ball rebounds from the front wall at such a sharp angle that it passes very close to your body as it approaches the short line, so your opponent will have a hard time tracking the ball. You just can't hit what you can't see.

Generally, it's preferable to hit the center V drive serve to the left, since that will be aimed to the backhand of your opponent (assuming you are playing a right-hander). Since the backhand is usually a player's weaker side, you'll gain an advantage by going for it. However, just to keep the receiver on his toes, you should, from time to time, blast one down the other side. That'll stop the receiver from getting into a groove.

The second type of drive serve, the wide V drive, is something of a gamble and should be used sparingly.

Start from the same position as the center V drive but hit the ball wider so that it bounces off the front wall and contacts the side wall as close as possible to the point where the short line meets the side wall. If the wide V drive is perfectly executed, it will squirt off the side wall for an ace, because it will be too low for your opponent to get a racquet on it. However, if you hit the wide V so that it strikes the side wall too high, the ball will pop out into the center of the court for a perfect putaway set-up for your opponent. That's the gamble. The perfect wide V serve will hit the crack between the side wall and the floor—a place known as the "CB crack" to the unfortunate opponents who've been on the receiving end of my wide V serve. By all means try the wide V serve, but keep it for those occasions when you are hot and need something a little special.

As with the other serves, I'm assuming you will hit the shot with a forehand stroke since that's usually the stronger side for the average player. However, if you have a good backhand, there's no reason why you shouldn't serve from the backhand side. This will probably add to the confusion of your opponent, especially if you can serve adequately from either side. As I've said before, variety is the keynote of the good server.

Drive Serve

1 2 3

How To Hit the Drive Serve For both the center court V drive and the wide V drive, take up a position in midcourt toward the rear of the service zone (Photo 1). If you stand too close to the front service line, you will not be able to take a step forward to transfer your weight into the shot without foot faulting. Bring your racquet back and drop the ball gently in front of you, so that it hits the floor at a point in line with where your front foot will be when you actually make contact with the ball (Photo 2). As the ball rises, start to step into the shot (Photo 3).

4   5   6

Bend your body preparatory to starting your forward swing (Photo 4). Time your forward swing to start as the ball begins to fall again (Photo 5). Move your hips forward to start the weight transfer to your front foot (Photo 6).

Drive Serve (cont.)

7

8

9

Swing the racquet forward and down smoothly (Photo 7). As your racquet approaches the ball (Photo 8) your weight should be mainly on your front foot.

Make contact with the ball just ahead of your front instep (Photo 9) and no more than one foot off the floor. Follow through in the direction in which you wish the ball to go (Photo 10). Here, I am hitting a center court V serve, so that the racquet goes out and across my body (Photo 11), finishing high on the opposite side of my body (Photo 12). Note that only the toes of my rear foot are touching the ground, showing that all my weight is forward; however, I'm in perfect balance, so that I can recover quickly and follow the flight of the ball, ready to handle my opponent's return.

10   11   12

You must be prepared to move quickly after a drive serve, since this serve usually results in a series of low, fast shots and the rally is over in no time flat. You should also be ready to get out of the way of the ball. Some receivers seem to make a habit of pounding a drive serve into the soft, fleshy parts of the server.

1. Hit the ball firmly and hard.
2. Make contact low and hit the front wall low.
3. Don't let the ball hit the back wall.
4. Serve to your opponent's forehand occasionally.

Checklist
for the
Drive Serve

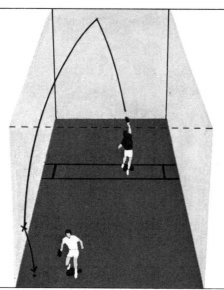

Fig. 2　High Lob

The
Lob
Serve
The lob serve is almost the direct opposite of the drive. It is a slow shot hit high to the front wall so that it descends along the side wall, brushing the wall before bouncing and almost dying very near the back wall (see Fig. 2). A well hit lob serve will not only force your opponent back to hit the ball, but the brushing action of the ball against the side wall will put spin on the ball, making for a more difficult return.

However, a badly hit lob serve may never touch the side wall and so will not slow down before bouncing and hitting the back wall. Such a serve will pop nicely off the back wall and give your opponent an easy chance to hit a winner.

If you are hitting to your opponent's backhand, aim for a spot high on the left of the front wall near the corner, so that the ball brushes the side wall on its descending flight. The key to a good lob serve is to get the ball deep to the back corner and yet still have it catch the side wall, so lightly that it does not bounce off into center court for an easy set-up. Done properly, the lob serve will cause your opponent to try an extremely difficult wristy stroke in an attempt to get the ball off the side wall.

As with the drive serve, you can hit the lob serve to either side. If you are going to hit a lob serve to your right, I'd advise standing a little to the right of the center court position to make sure that the ball touches the side wall on the right and slows down before hitting the floor and the back wall.

Lob Serve

1   2   3

How To
Hit the
Lob Serve
To hit an effective lob serve, stand near the center of the court (Photo 1). Bounce the ball fairly high (Photo 2), so that your contact with the ball will be about chest level. Take your racquet back as you would for a drive serve (Photo 3) and start your forward swing as the ball rises (Photo 4). Swing your racquet down and under the ball (Photo 5), keeping your wrist cocked (Photo 6), so that you make contact with an open racquet face (Photo 7).

4

5

6

Lob Serve (cont.)

7

8

9

At contact, lift the ball upward with a smooth, firm pushing motion (Photo 8). Putting a little underspin on the ball (Photo 9) keeps the ball on the racquet longer and will help provide a little extra control. Follow through in the direction in which you wish the ball to go (Photos 10 and 11) and complete your stroke with the racquet on the opposite side of your body (Photo 12). Resist the temptation to merely pop the ball off your racquet. ''Popping'' will barely give the ball sufficient momentum to reach the front wall. Hit firmly through the ball, so that it rebounds deep into the back corner.

10   11   12

You can bring off a rather tough variation on the lob serve by standing very close to one of the side walls and hitting the serve so that the ball rolls like wallpaper along the side wall without actually touching it. This is a very tough shot to return and a correspondingly difficult shot to hit well, so I'd recommend you use it only when you are pretty confident about your lob serve.

1. Pick a spot high on the front wall and aim for it. **Checklist**
2. Bounce the ball high so that you can bring your rac- **for the**
quet up under it.   **Lob Serve**
3. Hit the ball as softly as possible, to avoid popping it off the back wall.
4. Keep your eye on the ball.

The Garbage Serve If you are having difficulty with the lob serve, try the garbage serve—it's easier to hit and achieves almost the same results. In fact, it's such an easy serve that you can use it as a reliable second serve. The garbage serve is a lower lob serve that hits the floor close to the short line and then bounces relatively high into the rear corner (see Fig. 3).

How To Hit the Garbage Serve Start this serve over on the left side of the court, about five feet from the side wall. Bounce the ball fairly high and hit it with a lobbing action at chest height or a little lower. Aim to contact the front wall to your left about eight or nine feet off the floor. The ball should then rebound close to the side wall, bounce just past the short line and then carry over in a high, soft arc toward the back wall. Because of its high arc on the rebound from the wall, the ball will be at least shoulder high midway between the short line and the back wall where the receiver will be attempting to return the serve. There's not much a player can do with a shoulder-high ball except hit a lob or ceiling ball, which will give you plenty of time to get into position to make your next shot.

Ideally, the garbage serve should die before it reaches the back wall. If you hit it too hard, the ball will bounce off the back wall and present an easy opportunity for the receiver to kill the ball. Although the garbage serve is an easy shot, it does require a good touch to hit it well.

Once you have the knack of hitting the garbage serve, you'll find the shot equally easy on either side. Just keep it slow and make sure the ball bounces into the corner without actually making it to the back wall.

The Z serve—so-called because it takes a diagonal path across the court, striking three walls and the floor—is more complex than those I've just described, but no more difficult to hit. Basically, the Z serve is a high drive that hits the front wall on an angle near the corner, rebounds off the side wall, crosses the court to hit the floor near the opposite corner, bounces off the side wall and then dies near the corner (see Fig. 4). **The Z Serve**

The Z serve is an excellent offensive shot, provided you hit the ball hard enough so that it doesn't "hang" in the air as it crosses the court. A slow-moving crosscourt shot will be perfect for your opponent to blast at the front wall, probably leaving you wondering where the ball went.

To hit the Z serve, stand to the right of the center of the service zone. Bounce the ball moderately high and hit it at about waist height with a driving shot toward the left or right front corner. The ball should hit the front wall about six feet from the floor and no more than two feet from the corner. To hit the ball into the left corner, you'll have to stand facing the right corner with your left shoulder pointing toward the left corner. **How To Hit the Z Serve**

It is very important in the Z serve that the ball strike the front wall at the right height. If the ball is served too high, it will fly across the entire width of the court and strike the other side wall without bouncing. That's an illegal serve, of course. On the other hand, if you serve the ball too high but with too little angle, it probably won't reach the far side wall, but will bounce on the floor and then fly off the back wall. Another sitting duck for your opponent.

If the ball is served too low, it will bounce on the floor just behind the short line, allowing an alert receiver to run up smartly and smash the ball right back by your ear. Always aim your Z serve for a point between five and six feet from the floor and use about three quarters of your top speed. That serve will end up dying nicely in the opposite corner.

A good Z serve does require practice, so keep trying. Once you have the feel for this shot, you will have a very useful weapon for keeping your opponent guessing.

Four Common Service Errors

1. *Insufficient preparation*—Too many players simply step into the service zone and fire off the ball. That's two mistakes right away. First, it is quite possible to win the point with a well placed serve, so take your time and think before you hit the ball. Second, you have plenty of time to hit the ball. Pause, take a breath and concentrate on the matter at hand. You have control of the game at this point, so make the most of it.

2. *Poor placement*—If you are going to keep the advantage of serving, you must stay on top throughout the point. Why hit a badly placed serve that allows your opponent to get set and hit a good shot? Put your lobs close to the side wall. Keep your drives low. Make sure the garbage serves die at the back wall. Make your opponent do all the work.

3. *Hitting the back wall*—This is the cardinal sin of serving. If you bungle a serve so that it pops off the back wall, then you will get what you deserve—a good opponent will kill the ball and you will have lost the chance to serve. Practice your serves (you don't need a partner,

remember) until you can guarantee that your serves will die before they hit the back wall.

4. Admiring the serve—As soon as you hit the ball, move! Don't just stand there admiring the graceful arc of your serve. Bounce on your toes to the center court position just behind the short line and stay on your toes so you can move quickly to either side to take your opponent's return. Keep your motor running and put it in gear as fast as you can.

You should practice your serves regularly. Get out on the court by yourself with a box of balls and practice your entire repertoire. Experiment with different shots and find out what you can do with the ball. If you are having problems, ask a better player to watch you and tell you where you need improvement.

One final word: Variety. Alternate your serves so your opponent can never afford to second-guess you. You'll win more points by using your head than by using brute force.

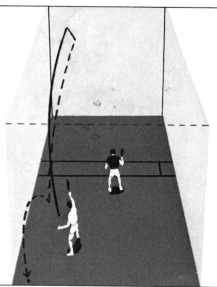

Fig. 5   Ceiling Return

The Return of Serve   When you are returning serve in racquetball, the dice are loaded against you: the server has complete control of the shot and commands the vitally important center court position. By contrast, the receiver has to diagnose the direction and speed of the ball almost immediately and play from a weak back court position. The receiver's main objectives are to stay in the point and try to regain the advantage. Thus, unless you are presented with a weak serve, your returns of serve should be defensive shots.

Although you can use almost any shot to return serve, the best return with today's lively balls is the ceiling-ball shot (see Fig. 5), which hits the ceiling a few feet from the front wall, rebounds off the front wall, hits the floor around midcourt and then bounces high into the back corner of the court where it dies. You can hit a ceiling ball with a lob stroke or with an overhead (see Chapter 4). The big advantage of the ceiling ball is that it forces your opponent out of the center court position and, if done properly, makes him return yet another ceiling ball. In fact, among good players, a ceiling-ball rally will result from a ceiling-ball return. Those ceiling balls will continue until one player hits a short ball or bounces one off the back wall that the opponent can then kill with a drive low to the front wall.

It's generally a good idea to hit your ceiling balls to your opponent's backhand so that you won't be giving him an easy set-up should you hit a relatively poor ceiling ball. A good ceiling ball will hug the side wall (sometimes called a wallpaper ball) so that the other player has to almost scrape the ball off the wall to make a return. However, don't worry if you can't do that with your ceiling-ball returns. Just keep the ball deep to the back wall so that your opponent has to retreat to get to the ball.

When you are preparing to return serve, you should stand about midway between the side walls and some five to seven feet from the back wall. I prefer to stand to

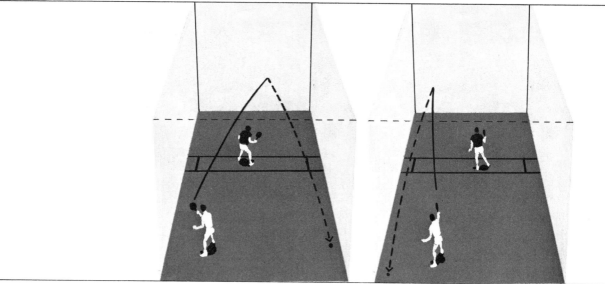

Fig. 6   Crosscourt Drive   Fig. 7   Down the Line Return

the left of the server, so that I can anticipate his actions a little faster. That takes some skill and experience, of course, but you may want to do the same. Remember that the rules say that you must be five feet behind the short line when the server hits the ball and, although you can hit the ball before it bounces on the floor, you must not cross the short line before you return serve. Of course, when you hit a ceiling-ball return, chances are that you will have to back up to hit the ball, so you probably won't be violating any rules. However, if you decide to hit a drive return you might be moving forward, so be careful.

You can use the drive return as an alternative to the ceiling ball when your opponent hits a drive serve, especially if the serve is not hit very hard and does not bounce close to the side wall. A hard-hit drive return to either corner will also force your opponent out of the center court position. The use of an occasional drive return will keep your opponent guessing and prevent him from anticipating your ceiling ball returns. However, remember that most serves will be to your backhand, so you should be fairly confident of your ability to hit a powerful drive from deep court off your backhand.

A drive serve may be hit down-the-line or crosscourt (see Figs. 6 and 7). For a down-the-line drive, hit the ball to the lower left front wall, so that it rebounds close to the side wall deep into the back corner. Don't angle your shot too much or it will hit the side wall as it rebounds into the court. A ball that pops off the side wall can give your opponent an easy plum. I'd recommend that you hit most of your drive returns down the line when you are playing a right-hander.

A crosscourt drive return demands a little more skill than the down-the-line variety. It's all too easy to misjudge the angle of a crosscourt drive, so that it hits the opposite side wall and pops off for an almost perfect forehand set-up for your opponent. Use this one very occasionally to catch your opponent unawares. The ceil-

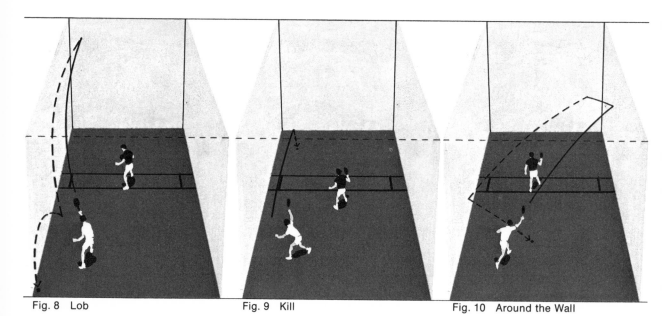

Fig. 8 Lob   Fig. 9 Kill   Fig. 10 Around the Wall

ing ball and the drive are by far the most common and the most effective service returns. The other possibilities are the lob, the kill, the around-the-wall ball and the Z-ball returns. All of these are fairly low percentage shots and should only be used when you are playing particularly well.

The lob return is very much like a ceiling ball that doesn't quite hit the roof. The ball is lobbed high to the front wall near the corner, rebounds close to the side wall, bounces behind the short line and then dies near the back wall (see Fig. 8). Unfortunately, with today's lively balls, most lobs will not die in the back court. Instead, they will rebound from the back wall, presenting your opponent with a nice easy set-up. Use the ceiling ball instead of the lob and you'll greatly increase the chances of the ball dying at the back wall.

The kill return is a drive hit so low to the front wall that it bounces off the floor almost immediately after rebounding from the front wall (see Fig. 9). A good kill return will hit the front wall so low that the server won't be able to get a racquet on the ball before it rolls out on the floor. The kill calls for power and accurate placement. It should be hit only when you have an almost perfect set-up, as, for example, when a hard-hit serve rebounds off the back wall. However, even when the set-up presents itself, the kill is a low percentage shot.

The around-the-wall ball is a somewhat higher percentage shot than the preceding two. This shot is hit crosscourt to the opposite side wall near the front wall, rebounds off the front wall to hit the other side wall at about midcourt and then bounces on the floor close to the backwall (see Fig. 10). A good around-the-wall ball will force your opponent out of the center court area. It is best hit off a relatively soft serve and should be hit hard enough to rebound off all three walls and still go deep in the back court. A gently hit around-the-wall ball will give your opponent an easy opening.

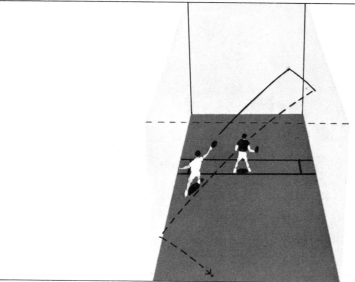

Fig. 11   Z Ball

Similar to the around-the-wall ball is the Z ball (see Fig. 11). The Z ball is hit crosscourt to the corner of the front wall, bounces off the opposite side wall back to the left side of the court, rebounding parallel and close to the back wall. A Z ball must also be hit hard and accurately if it is to go deep enough into the back court to force your opponent away from the center court position. I'd avoid using it unless you are very confident about your ability with this shot.

4

The Overhead
and the Lob

The overhead and the lob are the defensive shots used by most racquetballers. Overheads are hit to produce ceiling balls (see Fig. 1), thereby forcing the opponent to vacate the center court position in order to chase the ceiling ball back into the corner. Similarly, lobs are defensive shots that hit high on the front wall, bounce about midcourt and end up in the back corner (see Fig. 2). It's easier for an opponent to attack your lob, so it's not quite as important a shot as the overhead ceiling ball. Nonetheless, I think both shots should be in the repertoire of the average player.

It is possible, however to use the overhead as an offensive weapon—to hit overhead drives and kill shots. We'll take a look at those types of overhead in our discussion of offensive play in Chapter 5.

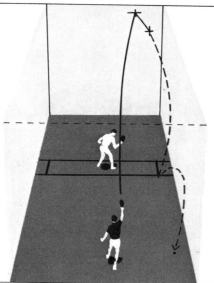

Fig. 1 Ceiling Ball

Using the Overhead for Ceiling Balls The ceiling ball has done more than any other shot to change the sport from a slam-bang, flailing and whaling game into one of patience, cunning and shot-making.

A ceiling-ball rally is racquetball's equivalent of the tennis baseline rally where one player waits for a short ball which will allow him to rush the net and take command of the point.

The ceiling ball can be hit either down the line or crosscourt. I prefer the down-the-line variety, in which the ball hugs the side wall as it rebounds from the front wall. This shot is almost impossible to cut off effectively, and your opponent will be forced to return the ball from deep in the back court with little or no real offensive possibility.

Despite my personal preference, you'll probably find the crosscourt ceiling ball easier and safer to execute. The ball should strike the ceiling near the center very close to the front wall (see Fig. 1) and the rebound will carry the ball into the opposite back corner of the court. If you hit the crosscourt ceiling ball too far over on the front wall, the ball will then hit the opposite side wall too soon before getting deep into the back court. The ball will then simply pop off the side wall for an easy set-up and a probable kill for your opponent.

I suggest you start by practicing crosscourt ceiling balls, then switch to the down-the-line shot when you have some confidence in your stroking ability. Of course, in play you should always mix them as the opportunity arises.

All ceiling balls hit from the back court should be aimed to hit the ceiling first. However, if you decide to go for the ceiling when you are caught in the front court, always aim to hit the front wall first and then the ceiling. If you hit the ceiling first, the angle will be so sharp that the ball will never make it to the back court. Hitting a ceiling ball from the front court calls for a lot of skill in judging the angle so that the ball will float down into the back court. Again, it's a situation you'll ordinarily want to avoid, so when you do try a ceiling ball from the front court, you should have plenty of confidence in your ability to hit it right.

Overhead

1   2   3

How To Hit an Overhead It is quite possible to hit an overhead off either side, but most players have trouble with the backhand overhead so I recommend that you concentrate on the forehand stroke.

The basic motion of the racquetball overhead is that of throwing a baseball or a football (if you've never done either, imagine you are serving a tennis ball). The racquet is taken back behind your head and then brought smartly forward to hit the ball when it is just ahead of your body. The wrist is snapped to provide extra power and spin.

4   5   6

Use an overhead when you realize the ball is about to pass over your head (Photo 1). With your eyes firmly focused on the ball, bring your racquet up and back (Photo 2) and begin to flex your body (Photo 3). Drop the racquet behind your head (Photo 4) until the racquet head is pointing almost to the floor (Photo 5) and your wrist is laid back and cocked (Photo 6). Keep your elbow high.

7   8   9

Swing the racquet up and forward as the ball approaches (Photo 7) so that you make contact (Photo 8) with the ball just in front of your body. Note that my racquet face is "open" (that is, laid back a bit, not quite vertical). This serves both to direct the ball toward the front ceiling and to put some spin on the ball by brushing under it (Photo 9). If I were hitting the overhead as a drive or a kill, then I would hit the ball farther in front of my body and with less of an open racquet face.

Notice, too, that my wrist snaps strongly through contact with the ball (Photos 8, 9 and 10). I then follow through in front of my body with the racquet finishing on the opposite side of my body. Don't just pop the overhead off your racquet with a short stroke. Remember, the ball has to travel all the way into the front court, bounce off the ceiling and the front wall and rebound all the way into the back court. Not only is that a long way for the ball to travel, but each time the ball strikes a wall it loses

10

speed, so if you hit the ball too softly you'll be giving your opponent an easy set-up in midcourt. Hit through the ball firmly and with a full follow-through.

A properly hit ceiling ball should strike the ceiling about two to five feet from the front wall and, if you are going down the line, the shot will be a wallpaper ball that hugs the side wall as it travels back from the front wall.

It's almost as big a mistake to hit the overhead ceiling ball too hard as it is to hit it too softly. If you hit it too hard, the ball will go back so fast it will pop off the back wall, ready to be flailed by your opponent. The secret is practice and more practice. If you have a spare court, try hitting a few ceiling balls to yourself. The ball takes long enough to complete its tour of the court that you can hit an endless ceiling-ball rally with yourself once you get the hang of it.

Checklist for the Overhead

1. Keep your eyes on the ball throughout the stroke.
2. Get your racquet back and your wrist cocked early.
3. Snap your wrist through the contact with the ball.
4. Hit the ball with an open racquet face to impart spin.
5. Use a full follow-through to hit the ball firmly.

Four Common Overhead Errors

1. Too Many Overheads—The average player, once he gets used to hitting the overhead, tends to overuse the shot. The only time to hit an overhead is when the ball is going over your head and you have no chance to wait for it to get low enough for you to hit a conventional drive. If you have the chance, retreat and let the ball drop so that you are not forced to use the overhead.

2. Hitting the Ball Too Hard—If an overhead is hit too hard, the ball will bounce off the back wall, giving your opponent lots of time to get set and hit a powerful shot. Practice hitting overheads until you have enough touch to ensure that your ceiling balls practically die in that back corner.

3. Catching the Side Wall—If you hit a ceiling ball so that it catches the side wall on its rebound, you will be giving your opponent a plum set-up. If you can't hit a wallpaper ceiling ball, then hit the ball down the middle of the court, where it stands no chance of catching the side wall. If your ceiling ball is going to die at the back wall, then it's no disadvantage to hit it down the center of the court.

4. No Follow-through—If you finish the stroke immediately after the ball comes off your racquet, you'll have little pace and almost no spin on the ball. The result will be a ceiling ball that doesn't get past the midcourt area on the rebound. Hit through the ball by using a full follow-through and you'll rarely hit a short overhead ceiling ball.

Fig. 2 Backhand Lob

Using the Lob Since the lob is a floating shot that should go over your opponent's head (see Fig. 2), forcing him to retreat into the back court, you'll need plenty of control to make this shot work for you. Now that the balls are livelier, it's all too easy to overhit a lob, so that it doesn't die at the back wall but bounces back into the court for an easy set-up. Some players prefer to hit an overhead ceiling ball instead of a lob in order to reduce the chances of overhitting. However, with practice, I think the average player can, and should, learn both shots.

In fact, off the backhand side, the stroking for a lob is almost identical with that for a ceiling ball, so you'll need to know how to hit a lob even if you use it only to hit ceiling balls off the backhand.

A lob can be hit either crosscourt or down the line. I favor the use of the lob close to the sidewall, which, of course, calls for the down-the-line shot. In either case, the lob is very much a defensive shot but one that can be used to put a little pressure on an opponent. In effect, a lob gives you breathing time to get back into center court position while forcing your opponent away from the center. Thus, your opponent has to go for a drive, giving you time to get in a good position to make an effective reply. In that sort of situation, many opponents will make an error. Therefore, I recommend the lob when you want to change the pace and put some pressure on your opponent.

Backhand Lob

1

2

3

How To Hit a Forehand Lob The stroking of a forehand lob is almost exactly the same as for the lob serve (see photo sequence on pp. 42–45). Simply remember to wait for the ball to come to you and make contact as high as possible. Use a firm motion, hit through the ball and follow through in the direction in which you wish the ball to go. Put your weight into the shot just as you would for a forehand drive. When you finish the follow-through, be ready to move to cover the center court position.

Since the backhand lob is more useful than the forehand, I'm going to describe it in a little more detail.

How To Hit a Backhand Lob In this photo sequence, I'm hitting a backhand lob before the ball bounces, which is also the way I would hit a backhand ceiling ball. However, the stroking is exactly

4   5   6

the same for a lob taken after the ball has bounced, except you should try to hit the ball close to the top of the bounce.

Before the ball comes near, turn sideways and get your racquet back (Photo 1). Shift your weight back so that it is almost entirely on your back foot (Photo 2). The forward swing starts with a looping motion (Photo 3) that brings the racquet down with an open face, almost horizontal, under the oncoming flight of the ball (Photos 4 and 5). Move your weight forward by pushing off your rear foot (Photo 6) and hit up on the ball (Photos 7 and 8), making contact with your arm straight.

Follow through in the direction in which you wish the ball to go (Photos 10 and 11) and then let your arm swing around naturally to complete the follow-through on your racquet side. When you finish the stroke, all your weight should be on your front foot (Photo 12) but you should be well balanced, ready to move for your next shot.

7 8 9

Checklist
for the
Lob

1. Watch the ball throughout the stroke.
2. Make contact with the ball just in front of your front foot.
3. Hit the ball with a slightly open face for control.
4. Follow through in the direction in which you wish the ball to go.

Four Common
Lobbing Errors

1. Overhitting the Ball—If you hit the ball too hard, it will travel too far down the court before it bounces and will not die at the back wall. Instead, it will pop off, giving your opponent an easy shot. Hit your lobs with sufficient control so that they bounce close to midcourt, no deeper, and will therefore be coming down sharply as they approach the back wall.

2. Too Much Angle—A sharply angled crosscourt lob will hit the side wall before it bounces on the floor. Such a

10

shot could be easily returned by your opponent. Make your lobs go down the line if you have any choice in the matter. Remember, the lob is a slow moving ball, so you can't afford to give it to your opponent on a platter.

3. *Too Low on the Front Wall*—A correctly hit lob should strike the front wall no more than three or four feet from the ceiling. If you hit your lob too low, it will not bounce high on its way to the back court. A low-bouncing ball can easily be taken out of the air by your opponent and that's the last you'll see of it in that particular point. Keep your lobs high.

4. *Failure to Recover*—Your objective with a lob is to get your opponent out of the way so you can regain the center court position. When you hit a lob, move. Your opponent will be leaving that center court open for you and you'll be getting out of the way of his return—and his racquet. Don't just stand there and admire your gracefully curving lob—get back into center court.

5

Offensive Play

A major reason for the rapid growth of racquetball is that it is both an easy and a difficult game to play. It's easy for the novice to go out on the court for the first time, hit a few balls and enjoy the activity. But the game is sufficiently complex that even after you develop an effective repertoire of strokes (and that can take some doing) you will find there is still much to learn about the placement of shots, the real strategy of racquetball.

I have a reputation as a crafty strategist, but I am constantly improving my own tactics and strategy. A player never stops learning how to play the game. So I'm devoting this and the next two chapters to strategy. This chapter on offensive play is complemented by the next one on defensive play, and then we'll go on to look at the special needs of doubles play.

Stroking and Strategy

Center Court Position The key to winning racquetball is control of the center court position: the area in the middle of the court just a couple of steps behind the short line. (It's the equivalent of playing at the net in tennis.) Not only is the center court the best place to hit winning shots, it is also the best place to defend against being passed by your opponent. In the center court, you are almost equidistant from all corners of the court, so that you minimize the time you'll take to get to an opponent's shot. With the exception of back wall shots, every racquetball stroke is possible from the center court position.

So your objective should always be to return to that center position and take command of the game. From the center you can control the pace of the game and thereby keep your opponent from gaining the center. However, you must use your brain when you are in the center court. Don't wait for the ball to come to you. Anticipate your opponent's shots and move accordingly. I'd be the first to admit that I'm not the fastest player the world has ever seen on the racquetball court, but I make up for it by covering the court.

Anticipation involves a knowledge of both the game and your opponent. For example, if I hit a serve deep to my opponent's backhand, so that the ball bounces at chest height when it reaches the back court, I know the chances of my opponent's trying for a hard, winning shot are almost zero. I also know that the chances of his hitting a backhand ceiling ball are very high, so I can edge over to the backhand side and be ready to move back to reply to that anticipated ceiling ball.

That, of course, is a simple situation where I have plenty of time to make my move. But suppose my serve is poor, encouraging my opponent to try a more aggressive response. If I've served to my opponent's backhand, I know he's more likely to attempt a down-the-line back-hand kill rather than a crosscourt pass. Therefore, I can edge over toward the backhand side, ready to move up to pick off the attempted kill. If my opponent is good enough to try a crosscourt kill, chances are he'll have the ability to hit a winner anyway, so I needn't really worry about that side of the court.

Of course, experience is a major factor in improving your anticipation. If you're smart, you'll ask yourself why you've won or lost each point as your matches progress. You can learn from both your mistakes and your suc-cessful shots. Watching better players compete is also an excellent way of broadening your experience. Watch how a better player serves and where he goes after each type of serve. Notice, too, how a player recovers after being forced into the back court. A good player will al-most constantly be on the move, never waiting for his opponent to hit the ball but moving immediately after taking each shot.

Conversely, you should always try to keep your oppo-nent guessing. Make life as hard as possible for him by using every shot at your disposal and never dropping into a pattern that he can easily anticipate. This means you must be able to use the three types of offensive shot—the kill, the pass and the drop shot. The kill and pass shots are both hard-hit strokes executed with a nor-mal forehand or backhand drive. They form the heavy ar-tillery of the offensive player's armory.

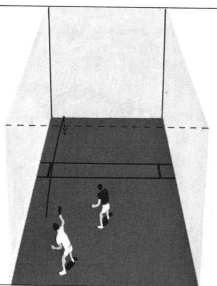

Fig. 1   Straight Kill

The Kill Shot

The kill shot is racquetball's strikeout. A kill shot is any ball that hits low on the front wall and bounces off so that it is unreturnable. A perfect kill shot is the flat roll-out, which hits so low on the front wall that it never gets off the ground on its return. If you wish to win at racquetball, you must have a variety of effective kill shots. When the opportunity presents itself, don't hesitate to use the kill and close out the point. With practice, you should be able to hit kill shots off both the forehand and backhand sides.

Naturally, there are risks in attempting a shot that places a premium on accuracy. The better the kill, the higher the risk of either failing completely or giving your opponent an easy set-up. If you hit the ball too low, it will skip or bounce before it hits the front wall—and you've lost the point right there. If you hit the kill too high, it will come off the front wall at the right height for your opponent to hit a kill or a pass. Chances are you'll lose that point, too. With practice, you can reduce the risk, but in the pressure of a competitive match those risks can creep up again.

There are four types of kill shots—the straight, the side-wall–front-wall, the front-wall–side-wall and the off-the-back-wall kill. The most common of the four is the straight kill (see Fig. 1). Among top players, more than seventy percent of all kills are hit straight, largely because the percentages of success are higher when only one wall is involved. I recommend that you concentrate on the straight kill, hit off either the forehand or backhand side, and leave the others until you've developed confidence in your ability to place the ball hard and accurately.

The key to hitting a straight kill is to hit the ball low. Wait until the ball is no more than a foot off the ground before you make contact. Bend your body and your knees so that you can get down to the ball. Hit it hard and low to the front wall. Aim about six inches from the floor and your kill shots will be too low for your opponent to get a racquet on the ball.

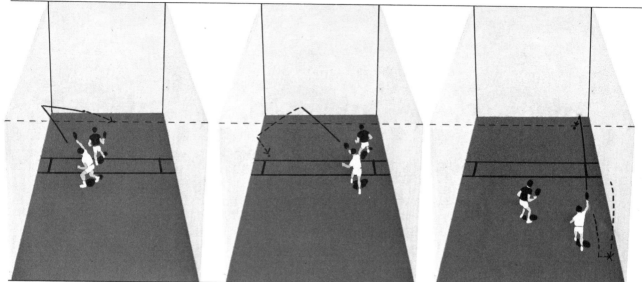

Fig. 2   Side to Front Wall Kill   Fig. 3   Front-Side Wall Kill   Fig. 4   Off-the-Back-Wall Kill

The side-wall–front-wall kill (Fig. 2) and its opposite, the front-wall–side-wall kill (Fig. 3), are used only rarely and then mostly when your opponent is out of position. For example, if your opponent is close to you and slightly in front, a backhand kill to the side wall first will keep the ball away from your opponent. Ideally, the ball should die as it comes off the front wall.

The kill to the front wall first is a useful maneuver when your opponent is out of position. Generally, the ball is hit crosscourt away from your opponent so that it bounces low on the sidewall and dies almost immediately. However, the front-wall–side-wall kill is a very risky shot, since it will often return to the center of the court if hit too high. Unless your opponent is very badly out of position it will present him with a perfect set-up.

The off-the-back-wall kill (Fig. 4) is not a shot that is used much by social players, although the top-ranked players have had much success with it. Handling balls off the back wall is largely a matter of timing and position.

Many beginners position themselves too close to the back wall, so that the ball is still too high to hit an effective kill shot. Wait for the shot to come to you and then hit it as you would a normal straight kill direct to the front wall.

Back Wall Drive

1 2 3

To hit an off-the-back-wall kill, let the ball go past you but don't retreat so that you are too close to the back wall. Stay at least ten feet from the wall (Photo 1) with your eyes glued to the ball. As the ball approaches, take your racquet back as for a conventional drive (Photo 2). Step forward to transfer your weight into the shot (Photo 3) and get down to the ball (Photo 4). Start your forward swing as the ball drops (Photo 5). Keep your wrist cocked (Photo 6) and your weight forward (Photo 7).

4

5

6

7   8   9

Hit the ball low, just ahead of your front foot (Photo 8) and follow through low (Photo 9). Stay down through the shot (Photo 10) and let the racquet complete its follow-through naturally (Photos 11 and 12).

This shot requires plenty of practice before you can judge the correct position and timing. Try it with your practice partner hitting you soft lobs that come slowly off the back wall. Remember to wait until the ball is low before you make contact. Patience is the key word here. The longer you wait, the lower the ball and the better the kill shot. You'll find that you have all the time in the world to hit a kill off the back wall once you have the knack of adjusting your position and timing the flight of the ball.

10

11

12

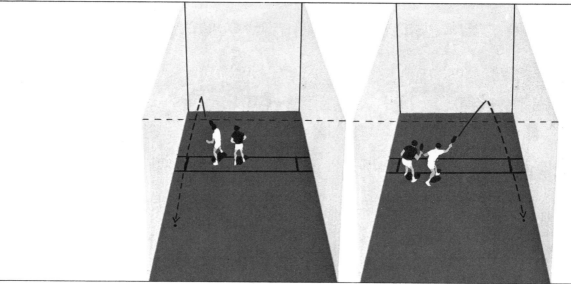

Fig. 5 Down the Line Pass Fig. 6 Cross Court Pass

The Pass Shot If your kill shots are often a little high, your opponent may sometimes move up to make a kill of his own or even a drop shot in return. This is a situation that calls for the pass shot. The pass shot is hit hard to come off the front wall and go past your opponent, thus giving you the point. A properly hit pass shot will leave your opponent standing wondering what happened.

As an alternative to the kill, the pass shot does not require great accuracy but it does require a measure of control. If you hit a pass shot too hard, it may not only pass your opponent but hit the back wall hard enough to rebound for an easy return. With practice, you'll be able to judge how hard you should hit to pass and yet not rebound too far from the back wall.

There are many ways of passing an opponent but only two that should be used with much frequency—the down-the-line pass and the crosscourt pass. The objective with a pass shot is simply to keep the ball away from your opponent. You might use the down-the-line pass shot when your opponent is in center court and you are near one of the side walls (see Fig. 5). Hit the ball so that it rebounds about waist high from the front wall and goes deep into the back court without touching the side wall.

By contrast, the crosscourt pass is best used when your opponent is out of position close to one of the side walls (see Fig 6). Aim your shot so that the ball strikes the front wall at about waist level and close to the mid-point between you and the farther side wall. The ball should rebound deep into the back corner, away from your opponent. Done correctly, the crosscourt pass will leave your opponent slightly dazed, wondering where the ball went. I recommend the shot against players who don't watch the ball carefully.

As with the down-the-line shot, you must control your crosscourt passes so that they don't come off the back wall or pop sharply off the side wall. Again, practice is the only cure for these problems.

Not every pass shot that you hit will be a winner, of course. If your pass shots do no more than force your opponent to scramble around the court making weak returns, then you will still be gaining an advantage—you can more than likely put those weak returns away with an easy kill. Although the pass shot can often be used offensively for a winner, it also has defensive value in setting up a situation where you can go for a winner on your next shot.

Fig. 7 Drop Shot

Unlike the pass and kill shots, the drop shot is not a hard-hit stroke, although it is usually a winner when done correctly. Use a drop shot when you are near the front wall and your opponent is farther back (see Fig. 7). If the ball bounces low off the front wall, move up rapidly and hit the ball softly at an angle toward the front wall. The ball should drop against the front wall and virtually die before your opponent can get to it.

I prefer to use the drop shot when I am up against a power hitter who is trying to kill the ball at every opportunity. The sudden change of pace forced by a drop shot will usually catch such an opponent totally unawares, so that he cannot get to the ball before it bounces twice.

The drop shot is a very carefully controlled stroke. Very little swing is required—you should almost try to catch the ball on your racquet and push it gently but firmly toward the front wall. If you hit the drop too hard, the ball will come too far off the front wall and your opponent will be able to run up and make a return. The

**The
Drop Shot**

drop shot is one of the few racquetball shots that calls for touch rather than power—especially with the lively balls used today.

A Warning Some of the top players—Marty Hogan, for example—play an aggressive game all the time. Hogan has the power and stamina to whale constantly at the ball and so force his poor opponents to play his game. Although it's fun to hit out at every ball, the average player needs more than an all-out slam-bang, aggressive game, because he does not have the skill and the stamina to keep up such a game. Use the lion-in-the-grass philosophy. Wait for the opportunity to come up, and then pounce. If you wait until the ball is in the right place, then you'll significantly increase the chances of hitting a winning kill or pass shot. Whale away at every ball and you'll start losing points and confidence in your shot-making ability.

A power player will often beat a weaker player on a streak of impossible kills. When that happens to you, wait it out. Sooner or later, the power player will lose his accuracy and you can begin to pile on the pressure. To do that you'll need a good defensive game combined with some aggressive shot-making. In the long run, an all-round player will be more successful than the power player. Concentrate on developing that all-round game.

6

Defensive Play

As I have emphasized in the last chapter and, indeed, throughout this book, control of the center court position is the key to winning racquetball. Virtually all your winning shots will be made from somewhere in the center court area. However, there will be many occasions on which you are not in the controlling position and have to play a defensive game. That is what this chapter is about: the defensive play that will get you back into that winning center court position.

Most of your defensive shots will be hit from deep in the back court while your opponent is in center court position. Your primary objective is to get your opponent away from the center and your secondary objective is to give yourself enough breathing space to get back into the winning center court position. Thus, the basic defensive shots are slow, controlled strokes that will allow you to place the ball carefully. Those shots are the Z ball, the ceiling ball, the lob and the around-the-wall ball. You should try to add each of these shots to your repertoire, but avoid becoming dependent on any one shot. If you have to play a defensive game, you must still have enough variety in your shots to keep your opponent guessing.

This particularly applies in the one situation in which I definitely advise playing defensively. If your opponent is on an unbeatable "hot streak," making one devastating kill shot after another, don't attempt to play his game. Use your entire armory of defensive shots, varying your placement and speed. This way you can put enough subtle pressure on your opponent to force him to start taking a few risks. Inevitably, those risks will lead to an error and you'll have broken the streak. Now you can change your style again and become an offensive player. Try it. If these tactics work for me, they can do the same for you.

Ceiling Ball

As we've seen in Chapter 4, the ceiling ball is hit most **The** often with an overhead stroke. It can be hit off either the **Ceiling Ball** forehand or backhand side (although the backhand overhead is a relatively difficult stroke for many players). It can also be hit with a loblike stroke as an underhand shot.

The ceiling ball is the bread-and-butter shot of the defensive player. It frequently leads to a continuous ceiling-ball rally with both players tossing up near-perfect ceiling balls until one commits a mistake that can be killed by the other. With the ceiling-ball rally, if one player hits a poor ceiling ball that either pops off the side wall or fails to go deep in the back court, the other player will be in good shape to hit a kill shot or an aggressive drive.

The action of hitting a ceiling ball (see Chapter 4) is almost exactly like that of pitching a baseball—if you've never pitched a baseball, imagine you are trying to throw your racquet at the ceiling close to the front wall (not that I recommend actually hurling racquets around the court, of course). If you've never tried this shot, practice it by yourself until you can keep up a ceiling-ball rally with yourself. Although the ceiling ball is not a particularly hard hit shot, you'll find this a pretty strenuous exercise, so don't overdo it the first time you practice.

On the backhand side, I recommend that you hit the ceiling ball as you would a deep lob. Use a full backswing, hit firmly through the ball with an inclined racquet and follow through as high as you can. Practice your backhand ceiling ball, too, since most good players will keep their ceiling ball rallies on the backhand side because that's usually an opponent's weaker side.

The Lob

As I noted in Chapter 4, the lob has fallen into disfavor with the better players because today's livelier balls often produce an easy set-up from a poorly placed lob. However, there are some signs that the ball makers are going to control the bounce a little more precisely, so perhaps we'll see a revival of interest in the lob before too long.

Despite the reservations of many better players, I think that the lob does have a place in the armory of the average player. The lob is a relatively easy shot to hit and it will gain you that valuable extra breathing space to get back into the game.

The lob should be hit gently but firmly with a high arcing stroke so that the ball contacts the front wall near the ceiling close to the apex of its flight. A good lob should rebound to hit the floor behind the short line with a high bounce so the ball will come down again close to the back wall but without touching it. A lob that reaches the back wall will often bounce off for an easy set-up. Similarly, a lob should not hit the side wall, so that it pops off into the center court. At most, the lob should glance off the side wall near the back wall. This will brake the lob's flight.

The lob is a very useful change-of-pace shot. If you are facing an opponent who is consistently hitting the ball hard, you can slow down that slam-bang style of play by hitting a high, soft lob. Your opponent may be so surprised that he won't be able to adjust to the change of pace and so may hit a poor shot.

The lob is very useful when you are in a tight spot. If you are forced deep in the court and have to scramble to make any kind of return at all, the shot to hit is a lob. Don't worry about style, just get the ball back high to the front wall. Such a lob will give you time to recover your position and stay in the point.

You can also try the lob when you are facing a good server. The lob may be hit off any serve. Kept deep, a lob will pull the server away from the center court and, most likely, force the server to return a ceiling ball, thus taking away most of the server's advantage.

Fig. 1   Z Ball Shot

The Z Ball   The Z ball, so-called because of its criss-cross path as it goes from front wall to side wall and then to the opposite side wall (see Fig. 1), is a relatively new shot that can completely confound an inexperienced opponent, but it is also a difficult shot to hit well and can easily backfire on you until you have mastered it. I'd suggest that you use the Z ball only occasionally and then only when you are in a good position to hit it properly.

You can hit a Z ball on either the forehand or backhand side, provided you are well behind the short line and quite close to one of the side walls. Hit the ball firmly and with power so that it hits the front wall near the opposite corner, preferably quite high and close to the side wall. The ball should then hit the side wall near the corner and bounce crosscourt deep to the opposite side wall, where it will rebound to come out into the court close to the back wall. A well hit Z ball will probably force your opponent to run around in a circle looking for an opportunity to hit the ball and finally hitting a weak shot that will give you an easy set-up. A Z ball will often catch your opponent going the wrong way and off balance: two ideal conditions for a weak return.

Don't attempt a Z ball until you have a good understanding of how the ball bounces after hitting two walls. Hit the Z ball badly and your opponent will gladly take the point. Hitting the Z ball properly almost calls for the skill of a pool player who can go around the table and still pocket the ball. A Z ball requires a similar combination of bravado, control, power and accuracy.

You will have to practice the Z ball to get a feel for the proper degree of power and racquet control necessary to hit this shot successfully. Remember that the ball must hit the front wall first, close to the corner. Remember, too, that a Z ball should not hit the ceiling or it may come down near the center court position, where your opponent can make an easy kill. When you can hit the ball so that it comes off the side wall almost parallel to the back wall, you'll know that you can hit a good Z ball.

Fig. 2   Around the Wall Shot

The Around-the-wall Ball

As its name implies, the around-the-wall ball almost makes a complete circuit of the court before being hit or coming to rest. Unlike the Z ball, the around-the-wall ball is hit to the opposite side wall first, near the corner and close to the ceiling. It then bounces off the front wall, near the corner, and goes crosscourt to the opposite side wall, bouncing off close to the back wall (see Fig. 2).

Like the Z ball, the around-the-wall ball is a source of instant confusion for your opponent, but it is also a shot that is difficult to hit well. Many players make the mistake of hitting the around-the-wall ball too hard, so that it also hits the back wall and bounces off for an easy set-up. It is also difficult to keep the around-the-wall ball high enough to prevent it from being taken out of the air before it reaches the last side wall. For these reasons, I think you should be very cautious about using the around-the-wall ball. Keep it for those days when you are hitting with lots of control and use it only when you wish to change the pace of the game.

Hit the around-the-wall ball as though you were about to hit a drive high to the side wall near the front of the court. The ball must be hit quite hard, but accurately, so that it contacts the side wall about three feet from the ceiling. Follow through high in the direction of the departing ball. Don't hit the around-the-wall ball so high that it touches the ceiling at any point during its flight. As with the Z ball, any shot that clips the ceiling will often come down in center court for an easy putaway by your opponent.

Practice the around-the-wall ball so that you can hit rallies with yourself, keeping the ball zipping around the court with very little change in your own position. When you can hit half a dozen around-the-wall balls in succession, then you'll know that you've developed the necessary skills.

Defensive Strategy When you are forced into a defensive posture, you'll need everything going for you to get back into the controlling center court position. Try to anticipate your opponent's every shot and quickly get yourself into position to respond to his next move. Even if you are tired after a lengthy duel, watch the ball and keep moving. Let me repeat that: *watch the ball and keep moving.*

When you are up against a player you have never faced before, use the first few points as a diagnostic test of what your new opponent can really do. Use your entire repertoire of offensive and defensive shots to probe the weaknesses in your opponent's armory. If your opponent hits a poor ceiling ball, then use your own ceiling ball to start a rally. That way, you'll soon be presented with a few easy set-ups. See which shots give your opponent the most trouble and calculate a choice that will maximize your own strengths and minimize his strong points. This may initially lose you a few points but in the long run you'll begin to force your opponent to play your game. Any opponent who is forced to play your game is going to lose.

Practice will make you a good defensive player. Most defensive shots can be practiced without a partner simply by rallying with yourself. Practice until you develop consistency and accuracy. When you can place the same shot several times in a row, you can work up competitions with yourself to see how far you can go without making a mistake. All defensive shots call for consistency and accuracy.

Remember, though, that defensive shots are not an end in themselves. Defensive play is simply a method of getting back into an attacking position from which you can win the point. It is sometimes possible to win at racquetball by waiting for the other player to make the errors, but in the long run the player who has an all-round game, who can use offensive and defensive shots and tactics, will win out over the purely defensive player. Use your defensive play to regain the attack.

7

Doubles
Play

There's a tendency among some young racquetball hot-shots to dismiss doubles play as an uncertified form of madness. "Too many people on the court, too dangerous and too little exercise!" cries the antidoubles faction. They couldn't be more wrong. Doubles play is fun. Playing doubles calls for much more mental effort and somewhat less physical effort than singles. Players of different ages and abilities can enjoy playing together. Certainly there's a greater chance of accident with four players on court, but I think that the risk becomes significant only at the higher levels of play where the action is faster and the degree of competitiveness is greater.

**Why
Play
Doubles?**

As the game grows, I think we'll see far more doubles play than we have in the last few years. Older and less athletic players will find that doubles is just as enjoyable as singles but less demanding. It is a more sociable game that a family can play. And, of course, four players can play more cheaply than two, since court rentals are usually the same whether singles or doubles is the game.

Picking Your Partner If you intend to play doubles regularly you ought to give serious consideration to choosing the right partner. It is not just a matter of finding someone whose game is similar to yours or who has complementary playing abilities. Doubles is a team game and therefore a doubles pair must understand each other and be able to communicate on and off the court without squabbling. If you are the kind of person who gets upset when your partner muffs a couple of easy ones, then maybe doubles is not for you. On the other hand, if you are the sort of person who can offer encouragement when your partner is playing off form, then you'll probably do well.

As far as playing abilities are concerned, the two members of a doubles team should complement each other—an aggressive player with a defensive player or a right-hander with a left-hander, for example. Much doubles play consists of defensive shots (long ceiling-ball rallies, for example), as well as waiting for the right opening to step in and kill the ball. Two aggressive players might lack the patience for doubles, but one aggressive player is useful for closing out the points.

Doubles Formations The usual method of doubles play is the side-by-side formation, in which one player covers the left half of the court and the other covers the right. All other things being equal, the player with the stronger backhand (assuming that both players are right-handed) should take the left side of the court. In the case of a left- and right-handed pair, the lefty will usually take the left court so that both players will be able to hit forehands down the side walls.

With the side-by-side formation there's no rigid demarcation line. If the ball is coming down the center, then usually the left side player will take it on his forehand (assuming again that both players are right-handed). However, if the player on the left is out of position, then, naturally, the closer player will take the shot. As I said at the outset, doubles play calls for teamwork. It's no good standing in your half of the court shouting "Yours!" when your partner is yards away from the ball. You should move together to cover the court. If your partner is forced to the left side wall to take a shot, then edge over to the left just in case you have to cover the center on the next return. If you are forced over to the right side wall, then your partner should edge over toward the center to cover for you. Even more than singles, doubles play demands control of the center court position.

An alternative to the side-by-side formation is the I, or front-and-back, formation. Here, one player covers the court in front of the short line and the other covers the back court. Generally, this formation works well only when the back-court player has a good defensive game and the front court player has a fast, aggressive game. The back-court player should also be able to shoot well from deep court.

If you are up against a team that consistently kills the ball while you and your partner are trapped in back court, then you may find that changing to an I formation for a few games will turn the tables. The front-court player will be able to get to some of the attempted kills and, most likely, be able to kill in return. And, of course, the mere change of positions may throw your opponents off their game enough to upset any hot streak they might have been enjoying.

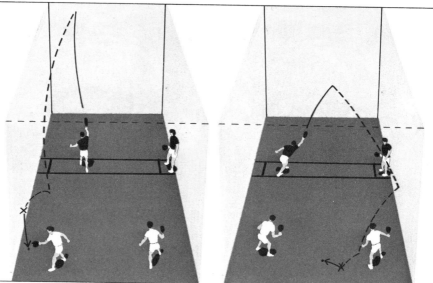

Fig. 1   High Lob Serve   Fig. 2   Drive Serve

Serving in Doubles When serving, a player will normally take up a position in the service area in his half of the court. The server's partner must stand within the service box in his half of the court. Note that neither partner may move until the served ball has crossed the short line. Before play begins, all players should agree on the order of serve and that order must be kept throughout the match.

If the first player serves and the team loses, then that side is out and service passes to the opposing team. If the opposing team fails to win a point, then that side is hand-out and the serve passes to the second member of that team. When the team loses for a second time, the team is side-out and serve passes back to the first team. Thereafter both players on each team continue to serve until the team is side-out.

The receiving team should stand in the back court about five feet from the back wall. After returning serve, both players should move up to try and take the center court position a few feet behind the short line. There's no requirement in racquetball that the server serve to a particular receiver, so either member of the receiving team can return the serve.

Normally, you will not win the point with your serve in doubles. Your objective should be to get the ball in play deep to the back court so that the receivers have to stay back and you and your partner can move to the commanding center court position just behind the short line. A lob serve that hugs the side wall (see Fig. 1) is useful on either side. Such a serve will usually start a ceiling-ball rally rather than generate an offensive return. A Z serve to the other team's weaker player is also an effective way to start the point.

The drive serve (see Fig. 2) is riskier in doubles since a hard-hit ball can often be returned offensively. Remember that a receiving doubles team will have both corners covered, so a ball that pops off either the side or the back wall will almost certainly be driven back hard. Even if the receiving team does not manage to kill the ball, the serving team may not have enough time to get into a good center court position to counter the attack.

If one member of the receiving team has a particularly weak shot—the backhand, for example—then most of the serves from both partners should attack that weakness. However, an occasional shot to the other partner will often produce a weak return, because that partner will not be expecting the serve to come his way. As in singles, it pays to mix up the serves occasionally and keep your opponents guessing.

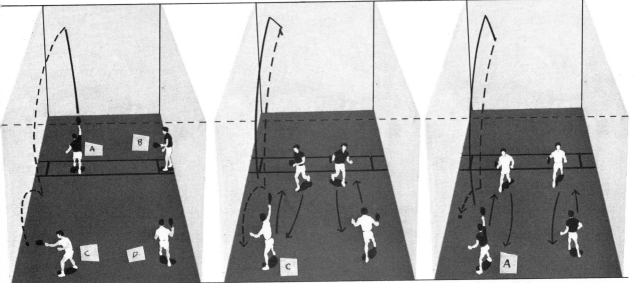

Fig. 3a Lob Serve   Fig. 3b Ceiling Ball   Fig. 3c Ceiling Ball

Good doubles play is like a ballet—the four players move **Control** continuously in and out of the center court position, **of Center** waiting for the opening to show. Poor doubles play is **Court** like a third-rate hockey game—lots of random movement with plenty of collisions and equally erratic shot-making. Keep moving on a doubles court and you won't come to much harm. Stand still and you will have a good chance of being hit by the ball, another player or both.

Let me show you what I mean with a simple doubles play. Suppose that the server (player A) hits a lob serve down the left side wall (Fig. 3A). As the serve goes down the side wall, the serving team (A and B) moves into the center court position. The receiver (C) drops back to take the lob and counters with a ceiling ball (Fig. 3B). Players A and B now retreat and their opponents move up into the center court position.

After he has moved back, player A hits another ceiling ball (Fig. 3C) and moves forward to take up the center position vacated by C. At the same time, players B and D

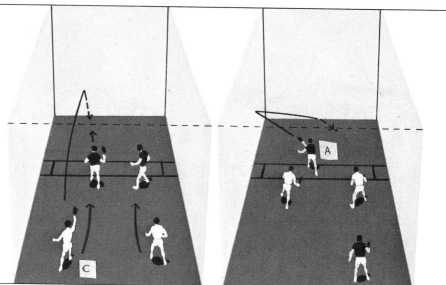

Fig. 3d   Kill Shot   Fig. 3e   Kill Shot

are also exchanging positions. A ceiling-ball rally ensues with the players moving back and forth each time the ball is hit.

Let's suppose now that player A overhits one of his ceiling balls so that it pops off the back wall and C attempts a kill shot (Fig. 3D). Player A pauses before vacating center court and then scrambles forward to take the unsuccessful kill. C and D move into the center court position and B retreats to cover the back court. Player A is now in a tough situation. He must win the point with this shot, since his chances of being able to force the other team back are very slim. So A hits a side-wall–front-wall kill that stays up in the front court (Fig. 3E), where it cannot be reached by the other team. Note that in this point the winning team had to be cautious—playing out the ceiling-ball rally—and yet had to take the risk of moving up to cover the attempted kill with yet another kill shot. It is this kind of chesslike maneuvering that makes doubles such a fascinating game. Don't be afraid—wait for the right moment and then pounce.

Another common strategy in doubles is to isolate the stronger player by pounding away at his weaker partner. Not only will the weaker players often deteriorate even further under this strategem, but the better player may lose his hot streak through enforced inactivity and hit badly when his turn comes. This strategy is all very well in a competitive match but I don't advise it in social play. Not only can it cause bad feeling between the teams but it can also cause dissension within the team with the better player berating the poorer for his ineptitude.

You should also consider varying the pace of doubles play. If the other team is scoring points fast, slow the game down by getting into position to serve or receive slowly. Call a time-out, particularly when the score is close. If you are ahead, speed things up so your opponents do not have time to collect themselves. Keep the pressure up both in the pace and action of play.

Watching the Ball   With four players on court, you must watch the ball carefully, not only so you are prepared to hit the ball when it comes to you but also to avoid injury should the ball be hit directly at you. When this happens, run, slide, jump or bend out of the way to avoid either injury or an avoidable hinder.

Keep your racquet up at all times so that you can use it to protect yourself if you can't get out of the way of the ball. I'd advise wearing an eye protector when playing doubles (see p. 132) to protect yourself not only from the ball but also from the other players' racquets. It's also important, especially in doubles, that all the players use the racquet wrist straps to prevent the possibility of a flying racquet hitting another player.

Doubles Can Help Your Singles   Even if you think you prefer singles play, an occasional doubles game can improve your singles game. Doubles play calls for some fast footwork from time to time and it can sharpen your ability to anticipate the ball's motion and direction.

When I play doubles, I am always conscious of my coverage patterns. Even if the ball is not coming to me, I move as though it were and make my decisions just as though I had to hit the ball. This can give you almost as much of a workout as a singles match.

Doubles also calls for the use of angles on both pass and kill shots. In singles, front-wall passes and kills are often good enough, but in doubles there are two people to be passed, so you have to use the angles to get around the players—very rarely will you be able to pass down the middle in doubles. Thus the strategy of doubles can improve your shot-making for singles.

I think you'll find, too, that doubles is a more relaxed game than singles, so your shots can be a little looser and maybe a little more imaginative.

8

Equipment

One of the great advantages of racquetball is that it is **An**
inexpensive. You need very little equipment to get out on **Inexpensive**
the court and start playing. In fact, a borrowed racquet **Sport**
and an old pair of tennis shoes are all you really need to
find out whether the game appeals to you. However, if
you're thinking of taking up the game seriously—and I
assume that you are or you wouldn't be reading this
book—it will pay to spend a little time selecting the right
gear. Unlike, say, a skier, you will not have to buy new
equipment each season to keep up with the latest fads. I
do suggest that you buy the best racquets and clothing
you can find—consistent with the state of your pocket-
book, of course.

For a start you'll need one or more racquets, some
balls, a pair of tennis shoes, shorts and shirts, wrist and
head bands and, perhaps, a couple of gloves. Let's look
at each of those items in turn.

Fiberglass Racquet

Selecting a Racquet

Since the racquet you use can have a marked effect on your game, you should try as many racquets as you can before you make your final selection. If your local club has a pro shop, chances are that the pro will have several demonstrator models you can use for a few games, either without charge or for a modest rental fee (often refundable when you make your eventual purchase). If not, borrow your friends' racquets until you find a model you like.

Your big decision will most likely be whether to buy a metal or a fiberglass racquet. There are wooden racquets on the market—generally imported from the Far East. Ignore them even though the price may be right. Wooden racquets are too heavy and unwieldy and they have a smaller hitting zone (the "sweet spot" in the center of the strings where the ball will come off accurately) than other racquets.

Metal Racquet

Personally, I favor the fiberglass racquets, as do most of the playing professionals. That's because fiberglass racquets are more flexible than the metal variety. This flexibility lets the pro stay in contact with the ball for a fraction of a second longer and gives a player more "feel" for the ball. That extra feel, for a control player like myself, is vital in placing the ball exactly where he wants it to go. On the other hand, in the fairly violent action of racquetball, even at the amateur level, it's all too easy to break a fiberglass racquet by hitting one of the walls accidentally.

Metal racquets, of course, are much stronger—you have to be something of an elephant to bend a well made metal racquet. However, metal racquets are stiffer than fiberglass and therefore some shots will lack control and feel quite abrupt. Some of the newer top-of-the-line metal racquets use an I-beam construction for the frame that seems to make it more flexible than the older designs. So, if you're in the market for a metal racquet, take a good look at those with I-beam frames.

The size of a racquet is specified by the U.S. Racquetball Association: the head cannot be larger than 11 inches long and 9 inches wide and the handle cannot be more than 7 inches long. The U.S.R.A. also specifies that the sum of the length and width of the racquet cannot exceed 27 inches. As a result of the specifications, there's not as much variation in the design of racquetball racquets as in the design of tennis racquets. I prefer a narrower head design, since that type seems to twist less in my hand when I hit an off-center shot. Many other pros prefer the more standard 9-inch-wide racquet. It's all a matter of your own preference and playing style.

Your racquet should weigh about 265–285 grams and be slightly head-heavy. The slight head-heaviness will help your wrist snap on most strokes. But be careful. A racquet that's too heavy will tire your arm and wrist muscles during a long match.

Most racquets come in only two or three grip sizes—small (4⅛ inches), medium (4⁵/₁₆ inches) and large (4½ inches). Most women and younger players will find the small grip size to be the best and most men will find the medium grip size to be most comfortable. In general, you should use a smaller grip size than for a tennis racquet because a racquetball racquet won't twist as much in your hand.

Racquets are sold with either rubber or leather grips. I prefer rubber grips because they seem to last longer and are easier to clean. Leather grips become very slick with perspiration after a few weeks of use and will have to be replaced a few times a year. Rubber grip models need only a periodic washing with soap and water to remove the skin oils that adhere to the rubber.

When you buy a racquet, check to see that the thong is firmly attached to the butt of the racquet handle. It's not only embarrassing to have a new racquet fly out of your hand during its first outing but it could be damaging to your opponent (to say nothing of the racquet itself). Check your thong periodically and *always* wrap it around your wrist when you play.

Most racquets are pre-strung by the makers, usually with a good quality nylon string at a tension of approximately 30 pounds. There's no real advantage in using gut for a racquetball racquet—the liveliness is in the frame, and gut will not add much to it at the low tensions used in racquetball. I personally have my racquets strung at the very low tension of 18 pounds for control.

Generally, the lower the tension, the longer the ball will stay on the strings, and the greater the player's control. On the other hand, the power hitters like to have racquets strung very tightly—35 pounds or more—so that the racquet acts like a trampoline. Unless you really slam the ball very hard, I recommend you stay with a tension of 30 pounds or less when you have your racquet restrung. A stringing job should last you most of a season unless you are very hard on your racquet. Getting a racquet restrung costs about the same as for a tennis racquet (around $10). It's worthwhile looking around for a store that's used to stringing racquetball racquets—or using the shop in your club.

A good quality metal or fiberglass racquet strung by the manufacturer should cost around $35. There are a few racquets coming onto the market priced at over $50. If the appearance of your racquet is important to you, then spend the $50—it won't do you any harm. Most racquets are guaranteed against breakage in normal play, for as long as a year for the metal variety.

When you have bought your racquet, take good care of it. Wash the grip from time to time to get rid of the perspiration oils. Check the strings to make sure they do not fray at the holes in the frame. If your racquet came with a cover, put it on to keep your racquet clean when you are not using it. Don't leave the racquet on the back seat of your car where it might be broken or damaged by strong sunlight. In other words, treat your racquet like the piece of precision equipment it is and you'll be repaid with many hours of playing pleasure.

To anyone who's been around racquetball as long as I have, the question of proper balls is, to put it mildly, vexing. In the early days, we had to use reject tennis balls without the furry cover. Nowadays there are several manufacturers making racquetball balls, but many of them are hardly better than those old reject tennis balls. You can take two balls from the same can, drop them both to the floor from about chest height and one will bounce a couple of feet higher than the other. At present racquetball balls are consistently inconsistent.

One ball is endorsed by the National Racquetball Club (the organizers of the pro tour) and another—from the same maker—by the U.S.R.A. As of this writing, those are probably the two best balls on the market, but the other makers are trying hard to improve their balls so we will probably see some big changes in quality and consistency over the next few years. As more people play

**Buying
a Ball**

the game the demand for better balls will mount and the makers will devote more time and money to solving the technical problems.

Right now, I can only suggest that you try out each pair of balls that you buy (usually they're packed two to a pressurized can), first by dropping them to test for consistency of bounce and then by hitting a couple of ceiling balls to make sure they have enough resiliency to bounce off the ceiling and come off the back wall at least four or five feet in the air. If the balls fail that test, return them to the shop and ask for a replacement pair.

Even if you hit on a satisfactory supplier of balls, you'll find that the life of a ball varies widely. Some will barely last out a game while others will stay lively for several matches. If you have a ball that breaks while still new, take it back to your supplier and ask for a replacement. If you have the time, a note of complaint to the maker might serve as a reminder that the quality of balls still needs improving.

Of course, the U.S.R.A. has specifications for balls, but they relate only to size, weight and bounce when dropped under standard conditions. There are no specifications for playability or durability or even for roundness. We can only hope that the U.S.R.A. will eventually devise tougher specifications and that the makers will comply with them.

Selecting Your Shoes In the rapid stops and starts you'll be making on the racquetball court, your feet will take a lot of punishment. Give them the best in footwear; buy a top quality tennis shoe with good heel and arch support. Go for comfort rather than appearance—badly fitting tennis shoes will raise painful blisters.

I usually wear leather tennis shoes, but that's a matter of personal preference. Canvas shoes are less expensive and often more comfortable if you have problems in getting a close fit. Most of the newer styles of canvas and leather tennis shoes have tread designs that will provide excellent traction on the hardwood floors of a racquetball court.

I suggest that when you buy a pair of shoes you wear the same type of socks you normally wear on court. In fact, I recommend you wear two pair of socks on court to ensure a tight fit and to help prevent blisters. Wear a thin

cotton pair next to your feet and a thick wool pair on top to absorb the inevitable moisture.

Speaking of sweat, if you play frequently, you may want to get several pairs of shoes and let each pair dry out thoroughly between uses. Not only will they last longer but your feet will appreciate a dry pair of shoes each time you play. Don't leave your shoes in your locker between matches. Not only will they not dry out, they'll almost certainly affect the locker-room air.

The Well-Dressed Player

Choosing Your Clothes In the early days of racquetball many players favored casually grubby court attire. However, those days are long gone. A number of equipment makers offer a line of clothing designed specifically for racquetball play.

Both men and women often wear a shirt and a pair of shorts on court, although more and more women are beginning to opt for tennis-style dresses or skirts. Tennis gear can be fine on the court, provided that the material breathes and allows you to perspire comfortably. However, you should also allow for more mobility than is usual on the tennis court.

I prefer a loose-fitting cotton shirt with wide, short sleeves. I also like the pull-on type of shorts—like the track athletes'; this style gives me greater freedom than tennis shorts. If you have a choice the shorts should be made from a double-knit material, since that will not absorb perspiration and cling to your thighs.

If you play in the cooler parts of the country you'll probably find a warm-up suit necessary. It's all too easy to strain muscles that have not been warmed up. A warm-up suit is essential if you have to wait without changing between tournament matches. It will stop your muscles from stiffening up and help you avoid getting chilled while waiting.

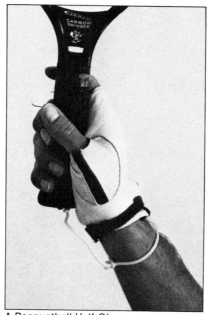

A Racquetball Half Glove

Other Accessories One of the biggest problems the average racquetballer has is perspiration. Racquetball is a very active game and even the most bumbling novice is going to sweat once he starts running about the court. I suggest you buy yourself a large supply of wristbands and headbands. Change them frequently during the course of a match to stop the sweat from running down your forehead into your eyes, or down your arm and onto your racquet hand.

Of course, your hand will sweat, too. If you find you cannot grip the racquet properly with a sweaty palm, try using a glove on your racquet hand. The glove will help absorb perspiration and give you a firmer grip. I prefer a full glove with a deerskin palm and a terrycloth back. Other players like a half glove that leaves the fingers uncovered; they claim they can get a better feel of the racquet that way. Again, that's a matter of personal preference. Try several types of gloves until you find the one that does the job for you. I take several pairs of gloves with me to a match and change them as they become soaked. You might try the same.

If you wear glasses on court, as I do, then a headband and a safety strap are essential. If your glasses fall off during a match, another player will almost certainly step on them. Your glasses should have plastic shatterproof lenses, of course, to prevent any possible eye injury should you be struck in the face by a ball or a racquet, or run face-first into the wall or the floor.

Contact lenses can be a liability on court. Many players wear them and do so successfully. However, they provide no protection from injury and can easily become dislodged during play. It might be wiser to wear your glasses.

Players who do not normally wear glasses might be

well advised to use some type of eye guard when on the racquetball court. Unfortunately most of the currently available eye guards are rather ugly and can even restrict your vision somewhat, although they certainly do give you maximum eye protection. If you can't face the thought of an eye guard, then a pair of glasses with plain safety lenses will do a slightly less effective job with a better appearance.

So there you have it. For the expenditure of less than $100 you can equip yourself in fine style for the racquet-ball court. Do it properly, look after your equipment and you'll play better. The player who feels comfortable on court and knows his gear is in good shape has a distinct edge over the guy dressed in a dirty T-shirt and grubby socks, wielding a five-year-old racquet.

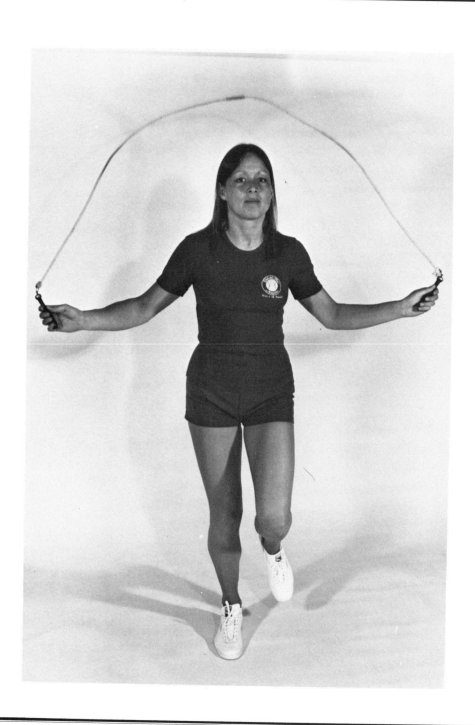

9

Conditioning

As we have seen, almost anyone can play and enjoy racquetball. Two players can have great fun on the court
even though neither may possess much physical
strength or stamina. Nonetheless, like any other sport,
the more you put into racquetball, the more you'll get out
of it. You will find it very worthwhile to get yourself in
good shape to play. In this chapter, I'm going to suggest
a simple program of exercises and running that you can
do daily, or at least three times a week, to improve your
fitness for racquetball. I'll also make some suggestions
for the more enthusiastic player who intends to enter
tournaments.

First, a word of caution. If you are an older player
who's starting to play racquetball for the first time, have
your physician give you a check-up before you start to
play and discuss the exercise program with him before
you begin any regular workouts. It is possible to overtax
your heart and lungs in racquetball play. If your physician recommends a gradual approach to the sport, follow that advice.

**Shaping Up
To Play Better**

Conditioning Through Playing I have always believed that the best training for racquetball is playing the sport. Racquetball is a fast, scrambling game with rapid starts and stops that place much stress and strain on the leg muscles. There's no other sport or series of exercises that can give your leg muscles a workout comparable to an hour or so of racquetball. If you have ready access to a court, I suggest you take your practice sessions on the court by playing.

However, don't go out and simply play your normal game; you are trying to improve your conditioning, remember. Get your partner to play a driving style of offense that has you scurrying back and forth, up, down and across the court. Both of you should avoid trying merely to kill the ball by hitting it low at the front wall. Instead, hit higher but equally hard shots in the hope of passing your opponent, so that he has to retreat and take the shot off the back wall. This passing style game will force both of you to run around more than in your normal game, thus stretching those leg muscles. Most likely, you will find yourself stretching more for the ball, improving your reach and giving your arm and stomach muscles a good workout, too.

I always try to stretch my body as much as possible in practice because there's an inevitable tightening of muscles due to nervous tension in competitive match play. By stretching my muscles to the limit in practice, I'm keeping my body flexible and, I hope, minimizing the reduction in muscle stretch that occurs in match play.

Concentrate, too, on moving in a fluid way. There are some players who throw themselves around the court trying to make impossible "gets." The end result of that kind of activity is usually a violent encounter with the wall or floor and, very possibly, injury. Strive to keep your balance as you move and be prepared to change direction with smoothness and grace. You will actually get into position faster with smooth acceleration and graceful changes of direction than if you throw your body recklessly around the court.

In the course of play, your arm muscles will also get a good workout, especially if you are trying to play a passing style game, which I recommend. In practice, concentrate on hitting through the ball (keeping the ball on the racquet as long as possible) and on using as much wrist snap as you can. Overemphasize the wrist snap and you will be strengthening the wrist and forearm muscles and helping the snap to occur more naturally during competitive play.

If you find your wrist muscles tire easily despite regular play, you can supplement your practice sessions with some additional exercises. Wrist curls with a light dumbbell are very good for improving flexibility and strengthening the wrist muscles. You can even carry an old ball around with you and squeeze it vigorously whenever you have a few spare moments.

If you prefer to stay in shape by playing regularly, I think you should play for at least an hour almost every day. If that isn't possible, then you should supplement your playing sessions with a daily program of exercises. If you intend to play in some serious tournaments, then daily play is an absolute essential. I often play for three hours a day during the tournament season, which is now almost nine months of the year. In the off season, I concentrate more on improving my stamina with a regular program of interval training.

Exercising Off the Court If you have only a limited amount of time each day to spend on getting and staying in shape, I recommend you divide the time equally between exercises to build your stamina and exercises to improve the flexibility of your muscles. As we've seen, you do not necessarily need to be very strong to play good racquetball, but you should have flexible muscles. The exercises I'm going to show you are aimed more at improving flexibility than at building muscle strength.

Distance running is not much help in preparing for racquetball play. If you already use distance running in a general fitness program, then I certainly would never suggest you abandon it. But if your time is limited you can build stamina and strengthen your leg muscles more effectively with stop-and-go exercising. Run a fairly short distance, say 200 yards, rest for 15 seconds and then repeat, with a slightly longer rest period each time. After a few 200-yard sprints, decrease the distance to, say, 100

Toe Touches

yards and then to 50 yards. Do the longer distances at about three-quarters of your maximum speed, gradually speeding up for the shorter distances.

This stop-and-go activity parallels the action of a racquetball match, where there is intense activity during each point with short rest periods as you wait for the next serve or slightly longer rest periods during the time-outs. Thus you'll be building your endurance and quickness at the same time. Start out gradually with a few minutes of stop-and-go exercise at first and build up until you can go for perhaps 15 minutes or so.

After the stop-and-go exercises your body should be thoroughly warmed up, so that, after a brief rest, you can go directly into the flexibility exercises. Do each exercise until you feel the muscles tire, pause for a few moments and then go on to the next exercise.

1. Toe Touches—With your feet shoulder-width apart, bend forward to touch both hands first to your left foot,

Side Bends

Sit-ups

then to your right. Straighten up with your hands above your head and repeat.

2. Side Bends—With your feet shoulder-width apart, bend sideways to touch both hands to the floor outside your left foot, straighten up, bend to touch your hands to the floor outside your right foot, and repeat.

3. Sit-ups—Lie on your back with your knees bent and your feet hooked under some heavy object such as a chair. Clasp your hands behind your head and sit up so that your right elbow touches your left knee. Next time, sit up so that your left elbow touches your right knee and so on.

Toe Raises

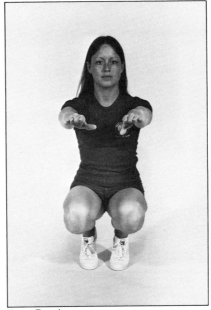
Knee Bends

Leg Curls

4. Toe Raises—With your feet together and your arms out in front, rise up on your toes and hold the position for a count of five. Lower your arms as you return to a normal standing position. Repeat.

5. Knee Bends—With your hands out in front of you, bend your knees until you are in a squatting position. Rise up again slowly. Repeat.

6. Leg Curls—Stand erect with your left hand flat against a wall for support. Lift your right foot behind you until you can grasp it at the ankle with your right hand. Hold the position for a count of five. Repeat on the other side.

Head to Knee Stretch

7. Head to Knee Stretch—Sitting with your legs straight out in front of you, touch your head to your knees, grasping your ankles in your hands if necessary. Hold the position for a count of five, then relax. Repeat.

Push-ups

8. *Push-ups*—Do several conventional push-ups with a straight body and legs, but push up with the tips of your fingers. This will help strengthen your wrist and forearm muscles.

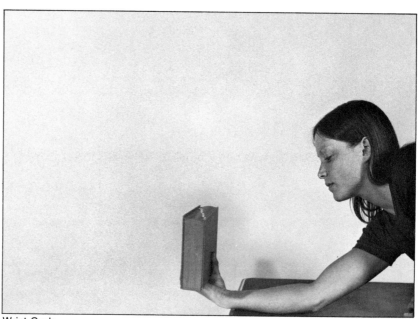
Wrist Curls

9. Wrist Curls—Using five-pound dumbbells or a heavy book, lay your forearm on a table with the palm up and your wrist overhanging the edge. Curl the dumbbell toward you, keeping your arm still. Relax and repeat. Do with both arms.

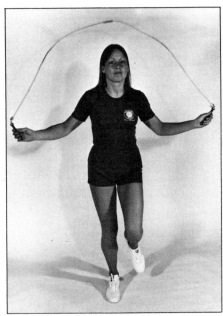

Rope Jumping

10. Rope Jumping—Skip rope in the conventional way until your leg and ankle muscles become tired. This is an excellent exercise for improving agility.

After the exercises, take a shower and relax, but stay warm and wrapped up until your body adjusts to normal activity. You may feel very tired after strenuous exercise, but a few minutes' rest will be enough for your system to recover.

Conditioning for the Tournament Player

If you are really serious about tournament play, you'll need a more rigorous program than the one I've just described. This may sound tough, but if you intend to play in an event that may have several matches over two or three days, you'll need to be in peak physical shape if you want to play your best.

For much of the time during a tough racquetball match your body will be functioning under an oxygen debt—what the physiologists call an anaerobic condition. How much your body can put out in an anaerobic state is largely a function of your oxygen capacity. However, you can build up your oxygen capacity with exercises that strengthen your cardiovascular system. These are the so-called aerobic exercises which are described in a number of popular and inexpensive books. Get yourself one of those books and start on a serious program to improve your oxygen capacity. The greater your oxygen capacity, the longer you can delay the onset of an anaerobic condition and the longer you can perform under that condition.

Your oxygen capacity is best aided by a program of circuit training, in which a sequence of exercises is performed without rest and with repetitions based on your capacity. Again, there are many books on circuit training, but I must emphasize that the program should be tailored to the needs of each individual. Setting up your own program without professional advice can be dangerous. If you work out at a gymnasium or health club seek out the advice of an experienced trainer there. Alternatively, ask for help from a high-school or local-college coach.

Once you have a program geared to your needs, stick to it. If you have to interrupt the program for illness or other reasons, go back to the beginning and start all over again. Test yourself every month and adjust the number of repetitions of each exercise and the circuit itself as your capacity gradually increases. Of course, you must combine the exercise program with regular daily play.

What To Do About Injuries

There are two major areas of concern about injury in racquetball—eye damage and muscle pulls. Eye injuries can be avoided in two ways. First, the player must watch the ball closely all the time it is in play. If you can see the ball, you can take evasive action when the ball is coming straight at your face. You can also protect your eyes with an eye guard. (See p. 132)

(See p. 132)

Muscle pulls can also be minimized in two ways. First, your muscles should be in good condition if you follow the flexibility exercises I described earlier. Second, you should always warm up for perhaps ten minutes or so before you play. Run up and down the length of the court with some rapid starts and stops. Do a few of the easier flexibility exercises to stretch your leg and back muscles.

If the court is cold, wear a warm-up suit during your pre-game exercises until your body is moving well enough for your muscles to be warm. This is especially important for your leg muscles, since the most frequent problem in competitive play is pulled calf muscles. When that happens all you can do is stop playing and rest up for a few weeks. Spend a few minutes warming up rather than a few days on your back.

If you do suffer a muscular injury, it's best to seek medical advice, of course. However, I've found that ice can be useful in reducing inflammation after a grueling match, and heat applied to a sensitive muscle before a match can postpone the onset of pain. It's unwise to play when you are in pain. Your muscle is sending you a message. Better pay attention and stop playing.

Some racquetballers suffer from tennis elbow and use a variety of elbow supports in order to continue playing. Consult your orthopedist on that problem.

Appendix

Official Rules
of the
United States
Racquetball Association

Part I. The Game

Rule 1.1—Types of Games. Racquetball may be played by two or four players. When played by two it is called "singles"; and when played by four, "doubles."

Rule 1.2—Description. Racquetball, as the name implies, is a competitive game in which a racquet is used to serve and return the ball.

Rule 1.3—Objective. The objective is to win each volley by serving or returning the ball so the opponent is unable to keep the ball in play. A serve or volley is won when a side is unable to return the ball before it touches the floor twice.

Rule 1.4—Points and Outs. Points are scored only by the serving side when it serves an ace or wins a volley. When the serving side loses a volley it loses the serve. Losing the serve is called a "hand-out."

Rule 1.5—Game. A game is won by the side first scoring 21 points.

Rule 1.6—Match. A match is won by the side first winning two games.

Part II. Court and Equipment

Rule 2.1—Court. The specifications for the standard four-wall racquetball court are:

(a) Dimension. The dimensions shall be 20 feet wide, 20 feet high, and 40 feet long, with back wall at least 12 feet high.

(b) Lines and Zones. Racquetball courts shall be divided and marked on the floors with 1½-inch-wide red or white lines as follows:

(1) Short Line. The short line is midway between and is parallel with the front and back walls dividing the court into equal front and back courts.

(2) Service Line. The service line is parallel with and located 5 feet in front of the short line.

(3) Service Zone. The service zone is the space between the outer edges of the short and service lines.

(4) Service Boxes. A service box is located at each end of the ser-

(Reprinted with the permission of the U.S.R.A.).

vice zone by lines 18 inches from the parallel with each side wall.

(5) Receiving Lines. Five feet back of the short line, vertical lines shall be marked on each side wall extending 3 inches from the floor. See rule 4.7(a).

Rule 2.2—Ball Specifications. The specifications for the standard racquetball are:

(a) Official Ball. The official ball of the U.S.R.A. is the black Seamco 558; the official ball of the N.R.C. is the green Seamco 559; or any other racquetball deemed official by the U.S.R.A. or N.R.C. from time to time. The ball shall be 2¼ inches in diameter; weight approximately 1.40 ounces with the bounce at 68–72 inches from 100-inch drop at a temperature of 76 degrees F.

Rule 2.3—Ball Selection. A new ball shall be selected by the referee for use in each match in all tournaments. During a game the referee may, at his discretion or at the request of both players or teams, select another ball. Balls that are not round or which bounce erratically shall not be used.

Rule 2.4—Racquet. The official racquet will have a maximum head length of 11 inches and a width of 9 inches. These measurements are computed from the outer edge of the racquet head rims. The handle may not exceed 7 inches in length. Total length and width of the racquet may not exceed a total of 27 inches.

(a) The racquet must include a thong which must be securely wrapped on the player's wrist.

(b) The racquet frame may be made of any material, as long as it conforms to the above specifications.

(c) The strings of the racquet may be gut, monofilament, nylon, or metal.

Rule 2.5—Uniform. All parts of the uniform, consisting of shirt, shorts and socks, shall be clean, white or of bright colors. Warm-up pants and shirts, if worn in actual match play, shall also be white or of bright colors, but may be of any color if not used in match play. Only club insignia, name of club, name of racquetball organization, name of tournament, or name of sponsor may be on the uniform. Players may not play without shirts.

Part III. Officiating

Rule 3.1—Tournaments. All tournaments shall be managed by a committee or chairman, who shall designate the officials.

Rule 3.2—Officials. The officials shall include a referee and a scorer. Additional assistants and record keepers may be designated as desired.

Rule 3.3—Qualifications. Since the quality of the officiating often determines the success of each tournament, all officials shall be experienced or trained, and shall be thoroughly familiar with these rules and with the local playing conditions.

Rule 3.4—Rule Briefing. Before all tournaments, all officials and players shall be briefed on rules and on local court hinders or other regulations.

Rule 3.5—Referees. (a) Pre-Match Duties. Before each match commences, it shall be the duty of the referee to:

(1) Check on adequacy of preparation of the court with respect to cleanliness, lighting and temperature, and upon location of locker rooms, drinking fountains, etc.

(2) Check on availability and suitability of all materials necessary for the match, such as balls, towels, score cards, and pencils.

(3) Check readiness and qualifications of assisting officials.

(4) Explain court regulations to players and inspect the compliance of racquets with rules.

(5) Remind players to have an adequate supply of extra racquets and uniforms.

(6) Introduce players, toss coin, and signal start of first game.

(b) Decisions. During games the referee shall decide all questions that may arise in accordance with these rules. If there is body contact on the back swing, the player should call it quickly. This is the only call a player may make. On all questions involving judgment and on all questions not covered by these rules, the decision of the referee is final.

(c) Protests. Any decision not involving the judgment of the referee may on protest be decided by the chairman, if present, or his delegated representative.

(d) Forfeitures. A match may be forfeited by the referee when:

(1) Any player refuses to abide by the referee's decision, or engages in unsportsmanlike conduct.

(2) After warning, any player leaves the court without permission of the referee during a game.

(3) Any player for a singles match, or any team for a doubles match, fails to report to play. Normally, 20 minutes from the scheduled game time will be allowed before forfeiture. The tournament chairman may permit a longer delay if circumstances warrant such a decision.

(4) If both players for a singles, or both teams for doubles, fail to appear to play for consolation matches or other play-offs, they shall forfeit their ratings for future tournaments, and forfeit any trophies, medals, awards, or prize money.

Rule 3.5 (e) Referee's Technical. The referee is empowered, after giving due warning, to deduct one point from a contestant's or his team's total score when in the referee's sole judgment, the contestant during the course of the match is being overtly and deliberately abusive beyond a point of reason. The warning referred to will be called a **"Technical Warning"** and the actual invoking of this penalty is called a **"Referee's Technical."** If, after the technical is called against the abusing contestant and the play is not immediately continued within the allotted time provided for under the existing rules, the referee is empowered to forfeit the match in favor of the abusing contestant's opponent or opponents, as the case may be. The **"Referee's Technical"** can be invoked by the referee as many times during the course of a match as he deems necessary.

Rule 3.6—Scorers. The scorer shall keep a record of the progress of the game in the manner prescribed by the committee or chairman. As a minimum the progress record shall include the order of serves, outs, and points. The referee or scorer shall announce the score before each serve.

Rule 3.7—Record Keepers. In addition to the scorer, the committee may designate additional persons to keep more detailed records for statistical purposes of the progress of the game.

Rule 3.8—Linesmen. In any U.S.R.A. or N.R.C. sanctioned tournament match, linesmen may be designated in order to help decide appealed rulings. Two linesmen will be designated by the tournament chairman, and shall at the referee's signal either agree or disagree with the referee's ruling.

The official signal by a linesman to show agreement with the referee is "thumbs up." The official signal to show disagreement is "thumbs down." The official signal for no opinion is an "open palm down."

Both linesmen must disagree with the referee in order to reverse his ruling. If one linesman agrees and one linesman disagrees or has no opinion the referee's call shall stand.

Rule 3.9—Appeals. In any U.S.R.A. or N.R.C. sanctioned tournament match using linesmen, a player or team may appeal certain calls by the referee. These calls are (1) kill shots (whether good or bad); (2) short serves; and (3) double-bounce pick-ups. At no time may a player or team appeal hinder, avoidable hinder, or technical foul calls.

The appeal must be directed to the referee, who will then request opinions from the linesmen. Any appeal made directly to a linesman by a player or team will be considered null and void, and forfeit any appeal rights for that player or team for that particular rally.

(a) Kill Shot Appeals. If the referee makes a call of "good" on a kill shot attempt which ends a particular rally, the loser of the rally may appeal the call, if he feels the shot was not good. If the appeal is successful and the referee's original call reversed, the player who originally lost the rally is declared winner of the rally and is entitled to every benefit under the rules as such, i.e., point and/or service.

If the referee makes a call of "bad" or "skip" on a kill shot attempt, he has ended the rally. The player against whom the call went has the right to appeal the call, if he feels the shot was good. If the appeal is successful and the referee's original call reversed, the player who originally lost the rally is declared winner of the rally and is entitled to every benefit under the rules as winner of a rally.

(b) Short Serve Appeals. If the referee makes a call of "short" on a serve that the server felt was good, the server may appeal the call. If his appeal is successful, the server is then entitled to two additional serves.

If the served ball was considered by the referee to be an ace serve to the crotch of the floor and side wall and in his opinion there was absolutely no way for the receiver to return the serve, then a point shall be awarded to the server.

If the referee makes a "no call" on a particular serve (therefore making it a legal serve) but either player feels the serve was short, either player may appeal the call at the end of the rally. If the loser of the rally appeals and wins his appeal, then the situation reverts back to the point of service with the call becoming "short." If it was a first service, one more serve attempt is allowed. If the server already had one fault, this second fault would cause a side out.

(c) Double-bounce pick-up appeals. If the referee makes a call of "two bounces," thereby stopping play, the player against whom the call was made has the right of appeal, if he feels he retrieved the ball legally. If the appeal is upheld, the rally is re-played.

If the referee makes no call on a particular play during the course of a rally in which one player feels his opponent retrieved a ball on two or more bounces, the player feeling this way has the right of appeal. However, since the ball is in play, the player wishing to appeal must clearly motion to the referee and linesmen, thereby alerting them to the exact play which is being appealed. At the same time, the player appealing must continue to retrieve and play the rally.

If the appealing player should win the rally, no appeal is necessary. If he loses the rally, and his appeal is upheld, the call is reversed and the "good" retrieve by his opponent becomes a "double-bounce pick-up," making the appealing player the winner of the rally and entitled to all benefits thereof.

Rule 3.10— If at any time during the course of a match the referee is of the opinion that a player or team is deliberately abusing the right of appeal, by either repetitive appeals of obvious rulings, or as a means of unsportsmanlike conduct, the referee shall enforce the Technical Foul rule.

Part IV. Play Regulations

Rule 4.1—Serve-Generally. (a) Order. The player or side winning the toss becomes the first server and starts the first game, and the third game, if any.

(b) Start. Games are started from any place in the service zone. No part of either foot may extend beyond either line of the service zone. Stepping on the line (but not beyond it) is permitted. Server must remain in the service zone until the served ball passes short line. Violations are called "foot faults."

(c) Manner. A serve is commenced by bouncing the ball to the floor in the service zone, and on the first bounce the ball is struck by the server's racquet so that it hits the front wall and on the rebound hits the floor back of the short line, either with or without touching one of the side walls.

(d) Readiness. Serves shall not be made until the receiving side is ready, or the referee has called play ball.

Rule 4.2—Serve-In Doubles. (a) Server. At the beginning of each game in doubles, each side shall inform the referee of the order of service, which order shall be followed throughout the game. Only the first server serves the first time up and continues to serve first throughout the game. When the first server is out—the side is out. Thereafter both players on each side shall serve until a hand-out occurs. It is not necessary for the server to alternate serves to their opponents.

(b) Partner's Position. On each serve, the server's partner shall stand erect with his back to the side wall and with both feet on the floor within the service box until the served ball passes the short line. Violations are called "foot faults."

Rule 4.3—Defective Serves. Defective serves are of three types resulting in penalties as follows:

(a) Dead Ball Serve. A dead ball serve results in no penalty and the server is given another serve without cancelling a prior illegal serve.

(b) Fault Serve. Two fault serves results in a hand-out.

(c) Out Serves. An out serve results in a hand-out.

Rule 4.4—Dead Ball Serves. Dead ball serves do not cancel any previous illegal serve. They occur when an otherwise legal serve:

(a) Hits Partner. Hits the server's partner on the fly on the rebound from the front wall while the server's partner is in the service box. Any serve that touches the floor before hitting the partner in the box is a short.

(b) Screen Balls. Passes too close to the server or the server's partner to obstruct the view of the returning side. Any serve passing behind the server's partner and the side wall is an automatic screen.

(c) Court Hinders. Hits any part of the court that under local rules is a dead ball.

Rule 4.5—Fault Serves. The following serves are faults and any two in succession results in a hand-out:

(a) Foot Faults. A foot fault results:

(1) When the server leaves the service zone before the served ball passes the short line.

(2) When the server's partner leaves the service box before the served ball passes the short line.

(b) Short Serve. A short serve is any served ball that first hits the front wall and on the rebound hits the floor in front of the back edge of the short line either with or without touching one side wall.

(c) Two-Side Serve. A two-side serve is any ball served that first hits the front wall and on the rebound hits two side walls on the fly.

(d) Ceiling Serve. A ceiling serve is any served ball that touches the ceiling after hitting the front wall either with or without touching one side wall.

(e) Long Serve. A long serve is any served ball that first hits the front wall and rebounds to the back wall before touching the floor.

(f) Out of Court Serve. Any ball going out of the court on the serve.

Rule 4.6—Out Serves. Any one of the following serves results in a hand-out:

(a) Bounces. Bouncing the ball more than three times while in the service zone before striking the ball. A bounce is a drop or throw to the floor, followed by a catch. The ball may not be bounced anywhere but on the floor within the serve zone. Accidental dropping of the ball counts as one bounce.

(b) Missed Ball. Any attempt to strike the ball on the first bounce that results either in a total miss or in touching any part of the server's body other than his racquet.

(c) Non-front serve. Any served ball that strikes the server's partner, or the ceiling, floor or side wall, before striking the front wall.

(d) Touched Serve. Any served ball that on the rebound from the front wall touches the server, or touches the server's partner while any part of his body is out of the service box, or the server's partner intentionally catches the served ball on the fly.

(e) Out-of-Order Serve. In doubles, when either partner serves out of order.

(f) Crotch Serve. If the served ball hits the crotch in the front wall it is considered the same as hitting the floor and is an out. A crotch serve into the back wall is good and in play.

Rule 4.7—Return of Serve. (a) Receiving Position. The receiver or receivers must stand at least 5 feet back of the short line, as indicated by the 3-inch vertical line on each side wall, and cannot return the ball until it passes the short line. Any infraction results in a point for the server.

(b) Defective Serve. To eliminate any misunderstanding, the receiving side should not catch or touch a defectively served ball until called by the referee or it has touched the floor the second time.

(c) Fly Return. In making a fly return the receiver must end up with both feet back of the service zone. A violation by a receiver results in a point for the server.

(d) Legal Return. After the ball is legally served, one of the players on the receiving side must strike the ball with his racquet either on the fly or after the first bounce and before the ball touches the floor the second time to return the ball to the front wall either directly or after touching one or both side walls, the back wall or the ceiling, or any combination of those surfaces. A returned ball may not touch the floor before touching the front wall. (1) It is legal to return the ball by striking the ball into the back wall first, then hitting the front wall on the fly or after hitting the side wall or ceiling.

(e) Failure to Return. The failure to return a serve results in a point for the server.

Rule 4.8—Changes of Serve. (a) Hand-out. A server is entitled to continue serving until:

(1) Out Serve. He makes an out serve under Rule 4.6 or

(2) Fault Serves. He makes two fault serves in succession under Rule 4.5, or

(3) Hits Partner. He hits his partner with an attempted return before the ball touches the floor the second time, or

(4) Return Failure. He or his partner fails to keep the ball in play by returning it as required by Rule 4.7(d), or

(5) Avoidable Hinder. He or his partner commits an avoidable hinder under Rule 4.11.

(b) Side-out (1) In Singles. In singles, retiring the server retires the side.

(2) In Doubles. In doubles, the side is retired when both partners have been put out, except on the first serve as provided in Rule 4.2(a).

(c) Effect. When the server on the side loses the serve, the server or serving side shall become the receiver; and the receiving side, the server; and so alternately in all subsequent services of the game.

Rule 4.9—Volleys. Each legal return after the serve is called a volley. Play during volleys shall be according to the following rules:

(a) One or both Hands. Only the head of the racquet may be used at any time to return the ball. The ball must be hit with the racquet in one or both hands. Switching hands to hit a ball is an out. The use of any portion of the body is an out.

(b) One Touch. In attempting returns, the ball may be touched only once by one player or returning side. In doubles both partners may swing at, but only one may hit, the ball. Each violation of (a) or (b) results in a hand-out or point.

(c) Return Attempts. (1) In Singles. In singles if a player swings at but misses the ball in play, the player may repeat his attempts to return the ball until it touches the floor the second time.

(2) In Doubles. In doubles if one player swings at but misses the ball, both he and his partner may make further attempts to return the ball until it touches the floor the second time. Both partners on a side are entitled to an attempt to return the ball.

(3) Hinders. In singles or doubles, if a player swings at but misses the ball in play, and in his or his partner's attempt again to play the ball there is an unintentional interference by an opponent it shall be a hinder. (See Rule 4.10.)

(d) Touching Ball. Except as provided in Rule 4.10(a) (2), any touching of a ball before it touches the floor the second time by a player other than the one making a return is a point or out against the offending player.

(e) Out of Court Ball. (1) After Return. Any ball returned to the front wall which on the rebound or on the first bounce goes into the gallery or through any opening in a side wall shall be declared dead and the serve replayed.

(2) No Return. Any ball not returned to the front wall, but which caroms off a player's racquet into the gallery or into any opening in a side wall either with or without touching the ceiling, side or back wall, shall be an out or point against the players failing to make the return.

(f) Dry Ball. During the game and particularly on service every effort should be made to keep the ball dry. Deliberate wetting shall result in an out. The ball may be inspected by the referee at any time during a game.

(g) Broken Ball. If there is any suspicion that a ball has broken on the serve or during a volley, play shall continue until the end of the volley. The referee or any player may request the ball be examined. If the referee decides the ball is broken or otherwise defective, a new ball shall be put into play and the point replayed.

(h) Play Stoppage. (1) If a player loses a shoe or other equipment, or foreign objects enter the court, or any other outside interference occurs, the referee shall stop the play. (2) If a player loses control of his racquet, time should be called after the point has been decided, provided the racquet does not strike an opponent or interfere with ensuing play.

Rule 4.10—Dead Ball Hinders. Hinders are of two types—"dead ball" and "avoidable." Dead ball hinders, described in this rule, result in the point being replayed. Avoidable hinders are described in Rule 4.11.

(a) Situations. When called by the referee, the following are dead ball hinders:

(1) Court Hinders. Hits any part of the court which under local rules is a dead ball.

(2) Hitting Opponent. Any returned ball that touches an opponent on the fly before it returns to the front wall.

(3) Body Contact. Any body contact with an opponent that interferes with seeing or returning the ball.

(4) Screen Ball. Any ball rebounding from the front wall close to the body of a player on the side which just returned the ball, to interfere with or prevent the returning side from seeing the ball. See Rule 4.4(b).

(5) Straddle Ball. A ball passing between the legs of a player on the side which just returned the ball, if there is no fair chance to see or return the ball.

(6) Other Interference. Any other unintentional interference which prevents an opponent from having a fair chance to see or return the ball.

(b) Effect. A call by the referee of a "hinder" stops the play and voids any situation following, such as the ball hitting a player. No player is authorized to call a hinder, except on the back swing and such a call must be made immediately as provided in Rule 3.5(b).

(c) Avoidance. While making an attempt to return the ball, a player is entitled to a fair chance to see and return the ball. It is the duty of the side that has just served or returned the ball to move so that the receiving side may go straight to the ball and not be required to go around an opponent. The referee should be liberal in calling hinders to discourage any practice of playing the ball where an adversary cannot see it until too late. It is no excuse that the ball is "killed," unless in the opinion of the referee he couldn't return the ball. Hinders should be called without a claim by a player, especially in close plays and on game points.

(d) In Doubles. In doubles, both players on a side are entitled to a fair and unobstructed chance at the ball and either one is entitled to a hinder even though it naturally would be his partner's ball and even though his partner may have attempted to play the ball or that he may already have missed it. It is not a hinder when one player hinders his partner.

Rule 4.11—Avoidable Hinders. An avoidable hinder results in an ''out'' or a point depending upon whether the offender was serving or receiving.

(a) Failure to Move. Does not move sufficiently to allow opponent his shot.

(b) Blocking. Moves into a position effecting a block on the opponent about to return the ball, or, in doubles, one partner moves in front of an opponent as his partner is returning the ball.

(c) Moving into Ball. Moves in the way and is struck by the ball just played by his opponent.

(d) Pushing. Deliberately pushing or shoving an opponent during a volley.

Rule 4.12—Rest Periods. (a) Delays. Deliberate delay exceeding ten seconds by server or receiver shall result in an out or point against the offender.

(b) During Game. During a game each player in singles, or each side in doubles, either while serving or receiving, may request a ''time out'' for a towel, wiping glasses, change or adjustment. Each ''time out'' shall not exceed 30 seconds. No more than three ''time outs'' in a game shall be granted each singles player or each team in doubles.

(c) Injury. No time out shall be charged to a player who is injured during play. An injured player shall not be allowed more than a total of 15 minutes of rest. If the injured player is not able to resume play after total rests of 15 minutes the match shall be awarded to the opponent or opponents. On any further injury to same player, the Commissioner, if present, or committee, after considering any available medical opinion, shall determine whether the injured player will be allowed to continue.

(d) Between Games. A five-minute rest period is allowed between the first and second games and a 10-minute rest period between the second and third games. Players may leave the court between games, but must be on the court and ready to play at the expiration of the rest period.

(e) Postponed Games. Any games postponed by referee due to weather elements shall be resumed with the same score as when postponed.

Part V. Tournaments

Rule 5.1—Draws. The seeding method of drawing shall be the standard method approved by the U.S.R.A. and N.R.C. All draws in professional brackets shall be the responsibility of the National Director of the N.R.C.

Rule 5.2—Scheduling (a) Preliminary Matches. If one or more contestants are entered in both singles and doubles they may be required to play both singles and doubles on the same day or night with little rest between matches. This is a risk assumed on entering both singles and doubles. If possible the schedule should provide at least a one-hour rest period between all matches.

(b) Final Matches. Where one or more players have reached the finals in both singles and doubles, it is recommended that the doubles match be played on the day preceding the singles. This would assume more rest between the final matches. If both final matches must be played on the same day or night, the following procedure shall be followed:

(1) The singles match shall be played first.

(2) A rest period of not less than one hour shall be allowed between the finals in singles and doubles.

Rule 5.3—Notice of Matches. After the first round of matches, it is the responsibility of each player to check the posted schedules to determine the time and place of each subsequent match. If any change is made in the schedule after posting, it shall be the duty of the committee or chairman to notify the players of the change.

Rule 5.4—Third Place. In championship tournaments: national, state, district, etc. (if there is a playoff for third place), the loser in the semi-finals must play for third place or lose his ranking for the next year unless he is unable to compete because of injury or illness. See Rule 3.5(d) (4).

Rule 5.5—U.S.R.A. Regional Tournaments. Each year the United States and Canada are divided into regions for the purpose of sectional competition preceding the National Championships. The exact boundaries of each region are dependent on the location of the regional tournaments. Such locations are announced in NATIONAL RACQUETBALL magazine.

(a) Only players residing in the area defined can participate in a regional tournament.

(b) Players can participate in only one event in a regional tournament.

(c) Winners of open singles in regional tournaments will receive round trip air coach tickets to the U.S.R.A. national tourney. Remuneration will be made after arrival at the Nationals.

(d) A U.S.R.A. officer will be in attendance at each regional tournament and will coordinate with the host chairman.

Awards: No individual award in U.S.R.A.-sanctioned tournaments should exceed value of more than $25.

Tournament Management: In all U.S.R.A.-sanctioned tournaments the tournament chairman and/or the national U.S.R.A. official in attendance may decide on a change of courts after the completion of any tournament game if such a change will accommodate better spectator conditions.

Tournament Conduct: In all U.S.R.A-sanctioned tournaments the referee is empowered to default a match if an individual player or team conducts itself to the detriment of the tournament and the game.

Professional Definition: Any player who has accepted $200 or more in prizes and/or prize money in the most recent 12 calendar months is considered a professional racquetball player and ineligible for participation in any U.S.R.A.-sanctioned tournament bracket.

Amateur Definition: We hold as eligible for amateur racquetball tournaments sanctioned by the U.S.R.A. anyone except those who qualify as professionals under current U.S.R.A.-N.R.C. rules.

Pick-A-Partner: The essence of the "Players' Fraternity" has been to allow players to come to tournaments and select a partner, if necessary, regardless of what organization or city he might represent.

Age Brackets: The following age brackets, determined by the age of the player on the first day of the tournament, are:

Open: Any age can compete.

Juniors: 18 and under.

Seniors: 35 and over.

Masters: 45 and over.

Golden Masters: 55 and over.

In doubles both players must be within the specified age bracket.

Basically racquetball rules for one-wall, three-wall and four-wall are the same with the following exceptions:

One-Wall—**Court Size**—Wall shall be 20 ft. in width and 16 ft. high, floor 20 ft. in width and 34 ft. from the wall to back edge of the long line. There should be a minimum of 3 feet beyond the long line and 6 feet outside each side line. There should be a minimum of 6 feet outside each side line and behind the long line to permit movement area for the players.

Short Line—Back edge 16 feet from the wall. Service Markers—Lines at least 6 inches long parallel to and midway between the long and short lines, extending in from the side lines. The imaginary extension and joining of these lines indicates the service line. Lines are 1½ inches in width. Service Zone—floor area inside and including the short side and service lines. Receiving Zone—floor area in back of short line bounded by and including the long and side lines.

Three-Wall—**Serve**—A serve that goes beyond the side walls on the fly is player or side out. A serve that goes beyond the long line on a fly but within the side walls is the same as a "short."

**ONE-WALL
AND
THREE-WALL
RULES**

Index